STAY EXTRAORDINARY!

UNLEASHINGYOURHERO.COM

Unleashing Your Hero

"Heroes are everywhere, and Kevin Brown's gift and message of hope is helping people realize that they can be heroes too!"

—Commander Mary Kelly, US Navy,
Author of *The Five Minute Leadership Guide*

"*Unleashing Your Hero* will help you create magic in business and in life. Kevin Brown is a captivating and relatable storyteller (I've seen him receive two standing ovations from a room full of high achievers). I found many similarities to my own life experience and one powerful truth we share . . . in our brokenness, we can help others find their wholeness."

—Jon Dorenbos,
America's Got Talent Finalist, Magician,
Former NFL Pro Bowler, and Author of *Life Is Magic*

"Kevin Brown is living his purpose and creating a legacy of people making a difference with their lives. He retired from a successful executive career to do what God called him to do: to touch people's hearts with humor, inspiration, and an action plan for changing their futures by serving others graciously. Kevin is living his message, and I know you'll be inspired by his work!"

—Richard A. Isaacson,
CEO at SERVPRO®

"It is a rare thing to be in the presence of someone who can truly see through our broken human façades and touch the foundation of our humanity . . . the soul! Kevin Brown in *Unleashing Your Hero* commands your attention with words so vulnerable at times you crumble. Immediately, his openness turns into power and action, with a plan designed to put you back together. Not only to make you whole again but to provide a rebirth as a new creation, the best of you, the hero within! Thank you, Kevin, for helping me unleash the hero inside and giving me hope to be my best for others every single day."

—Ben Utecht,
XLI Super Bowl Champion and 2019
Tony Dungy Uncommon Leader Award Winner

"Kevin Brown's *Unleashing Your Hero* is a roadmap to the little Superman in each of us!"

—John Ondrasik (Five For Fighting)

"Raw, relatable, and relevant is how I describe this masterpiece. *Unleashing Your Hero* is a gift that empowers you to be a better person and create a better life. You will be captivated by Kevin Brown's storytelling and experience a shift in your mindset. I love this book and can't wait to see it become a movie. Kevin, Josh, and Lisa, thank you for giving the world hope to cope."

—Dr. Simon T. Bailey, DBA, CSP, CPAE,
Motivational Speaker and Author

UNLEASHING YOUR HERO

Rise Above Any Challenge, Expand Your Impact, and Be the Hero the World Needs

• • •

KEVIN D. BROWN

HARPERCOLLINS
LEADERSHIP

AN IMPRINT OF HARPERCOLLINS

To Lisa.
The one who brings out the best in me, has endured the worst of me,
and somehow, through it all, still loves me.
I love you back, Wonder Woman.

•   •   •

Published by Harper Horizon, an imprint of HarperCollins Focus LLC.
Any internet addresses, phone numbers, or company or product information printed in this
book are offered as a resource and are not intended in any way to be or to imply an endorsement by Harper Horizon, nor does Harper Horizon vouch for the existence, content, or services
of these sites, phone numbers, companies, or products beyond the life of this book.

ISBN 978-1-4002-2877-5 (eBook)
ISBN 978-1-4002-2876-8 (HC)

Library of Congress Control Number: 2021942661

Text design by Maria E. Torres, Neuwirth & Associates, Inc.

Printed in Italy
21 22 23 24 25   GV 10 9 8 7 6 5 4 3 2 1

• CONTENTS •

FOREWORD BY DAVID COTTRELL • vii

INTRODUCTION: The World Needs Heroes • ix

CHAPTER 1: Running from Demons 1

CHAPTER 2: Running Toward a Purpose 23

CHAPTER 3: Mutual Healing 41

CHAPTER 4: Wonder Woman to the Rescue 47

CHAPTER 5: Disaster Recovery and Restoration 63

CHAPTER 6: Searching for Heroes 73

CHAPTER 7: The Everyday Heroes Among Us 93

CHAPTER 8: Josh-Brown and "Aunt Bea" 109

CHAPTER 9: A Lasting Impression 131

CHAPTER 10: A Big Bold Leap 147

CHAPTER 11: Putting On the Cape 167

CHAPTER 12: A Heroic Legacy 183

ACKNOWLEDGMENTS • 197

ABOUT THE AUTHOR • 198

Seldom in my life have I been as inspired and moved by a book as I have with the uplifting work you are reading or listening to right now.

I am willing to bet you will say the same when you are finished.

Sprouting from a sheet of yellow notepad paper with one handwritten word on it—HERO—is the true-life story of my friend Kevin Brown.

Why is Kevin's story so engaging to everyone who reads his words or listens to him speak? I think it is because he is one of us, an everyday person who has prospered through some very tough times. His message is one that each of us can relate to.

Unleashing Your Hero begins with the story of Kevin's journey back from a lost life that resulted from a horrendous experience in his boy-hood. The road he was on ultimately led to a dead end, but with the help of a few heroes, Kevin turned it into a new beginning. This cast of heroes helped him with the arduous task of reclaiming a life that had spiraled out of control for a decade.

One of the heroes you will meet is his wife, Lisa. A calm, positive, loving woman who provided Kevin with insights that helped him rec-ognize and accept support and guidance. Lisa encouraged him to look beyond the image reflected in his mirror. She encouraged him to see those encouragers lined up behind him. Her simple advice was for Kevin to share his heroes' stories.

This book is also about apple pancakes. That may not sound like something to write a book about, but don't make that judgment until you read the story. *Unleashing Your Hero* introduces us to an incredible young man and his relationship with his parents and a chef named Bea. You will discover how one person positively influenced the life of an entire family. Bea is also an example of someone who, in serving others, reaped substantial benefits along the way. In fact, her efforts led to positive change throughout what was already a huge, successful organization.

Kevin Brown is one of my heroes. The HERO acronym that Kevin introduces us to in this book describes why he is my hero.

Kevin is one of the most **h**elpful people I have ever met. He is interested in making all of our lives better and, with his words and wisdom, has provided inspiration to help us become our very best.

Kevin is **e**xceptional. He is a master storyteller and one of the best speakers on the planet. His message is sincere, moving, and encouraging.

Kevin is **r**esponsible. I especially admire that trait about him. When he says that he is going to do something, you can consider it done.

Kevin is **o**ptimistic. Life has not always been a bowl of cherries for Kevin. He has overcome obstacles that most of us will never have to face. He lives life to the fullest.

Unleashing Your Hero is about a man who overcame the heartbreak of a broken childhood, homelessness, and helplessness to become a person of amazing influence.

I am grateful for Kevin's message of hope. His words will help encourage, inspire, and motivate you to become the person you want to be.

Finally, this is a book that you will want to share with anyone who needs a hero at any stage of life. Enjoy Kevin's message just as you would savor an extra-large plate of apple pancakes covered in warm syrup. It is that good.

Then, pass it on.

David Cottrell
Author of *Monday Morning Leadership*
and *Quit Drifting, Lift the Fog, and Get Lucky*
Boerne, Texas

The World Needs Heroes

The question I am most often asked after my speeches to corporations and organizations (besides "How did you get such a beautiful person to marry you?") is this:

"How does a guy with a ninth-grade education make his way from homelessness to the executive boardroom while helping to build a multibillion-dollar brand?"

The follow-up is often: "How does that same guy find his way back from a life that was littered with broken promises, failed relationships, and burned bridges?"

Great questions.

I've asked myself the same things many times.

When my life was spiraling out of control as a young man, I had no vision of myself sitting in an executive suite on a high-back leather chair at a large mahogany table.

My only goal, many nights, was to find food and a safe place to sleep.

Looking back, those memories seem like they are from the life of another person. I suppose it was someone else. The person I had become. Back then, I was convinced that I was no good. There were more than a few willing to confirm that notion for me.

Then I found a friend, or that friend found me. His journey had followed a similar path of frustration and failure, but he had overcome his challenges, turned his life around, and found success professionally and personally.

One day, he scribbled something on a piece of paper, handed it to me, and told me, "These words changed my life."

Those words were: "Nothing changed. I changed. Everything changed."

He helped me see that achieving success at work and in life is not complicated. Be your best. Do your best. Serve others well.

If you put those words into action, you will be well on your way to a better and more fulfilling life.

You know that already, I'm sure. But we can get lost sometimes.

The stress and pressures of business and life pile on. We lose focus. Our confidence disintegrates. We neglect our gifts and accept whatever happens to us.

What happened to me in my adolescence was horrific, and I became a lost boy at thirteen years old. I believed I had nowhere to turn and that no one would understand. I made one bad choice after another.

I lost hope.

I eventually walled off the suffering boy, but that left a young man with not a clue about who he was or where he was headed.

Thankfully, someone found me wandering in the wilderness and helped me find a path. A real-life hero recognized my distress and took the time to save a struggling street kid. More heroes came along to encourage and support me.

This book is about welcoming heroes into your life and then becoming a hero in the lives of others. I learned lessons that apply to both our personal and professional lives.

My story is about redemption, forgiveness, and grace.

It's about brand building, customer excellence, and leadership.

In sharing my story of the heroes I've encountered, my goal is to elevate your life and encourage you to bring the best version of yourself to every moment you live.

The world needs heroes, but by that I don't mean we need alarmingly muscular people running around wearing tights and a cape. (Unless you're into that.)

Instead, the world needs heroes who are just like you. And if you are alarmingly muscular, that's okay.

1

RUNNING FROM DEMONS

ON A FRIGID MICHIGAN NIGHT, clear skies gave way to clouds hanging over me. It seemed unusually cold. Perhaps that was the hopelessness setting in.

I wanted to die.

There was nothing left in this life for me. I had reached bottom—drowning in the deep end, filled with self-destruction, self-loathing, and my own stupidity. Demons that had chased me since I was a teenager now had a death grip on me. I was living in my car. There was no place left to turn.

The only question on that night was whether to steal some food or just end things once and for all.

I wanted to end the pain. But the coward in me couldn't do it. I didn't have the courage to take my own life. I prayed a killer might come along in the darkness and do it for me. Those prayers went unanswered.

If I couldn't end my life, I had to figure out how to change it. To stick around, I had to stop the downward spiral. But how? I wanted to believe a better life was possible for me. I just didn't know where or how to turn it around.

As I drifted into an uneasy sleep, my mind went back to better days, before I'd lost my way. When I was a boy, my family went on vacations that were only a few miles from home because we didn't have any money to go farther away. Today, they'd probably be considered "staycations."

Often, my dad would rent a friend's cottage on a lake near Fremont, less than thirty miles from our home in Muskegon. My dad and my older brother were more into fishing than I was, but I always wanted to go out on the water with them.

They thought I was too much of a pain in the butt because I couldn't swim and had a serious fear of falling into the lake and drowning.

"You talk too much and it scares the fish," my father often said. "You can fish off the dock while we go out. It's safer there, anyway."

So one morning when I was seven years old, I went out to the dock by myself after my dad and brother had rowed out on the lake. I had a junior-size rod and reel, a tiny tackle box, and a Styrofoam cup full of slimy, smelly worms.

I wore a bucket hat and, because I was Mr. Safety First, an orange life vest. I pretended to be a serious fisherman, casting and reeling like I was using a lure instead of letting my poor worm just sink to the bottom.

I liked casting. It made me feel like a pro. I thought my dad and brother might be impressed enough to one day let me in the boat with them.

After a few warmups, I decided to see how far I could cast. I raised the pole over my head and kept pushing it back until the rod was parallel to the ground, and then I whipped that worm way out into the lake.

To my shock, I hooked something. At first it felt like a major lunker, a mighty whopper that would feed my family for a week or take up a huge space over the fireplace, if we had a fireplace.

But then, as I yanked the line and found myself going headfirst off the dock, I realized I had taken my pole so far back that I'd hooked the back of my own life preserver and had whipped myself into the lake.

My dad and my brother heard the splash and began rowing, but they were a long way out.

"Hang on, Kevin, we're coming!" Dad yelled.

I was flailing and screaming, terrified of drowning.

My grandma and grandpa were with us that year, and grandma came a-running out of the cabin as fast as her ol' legs could go.

Once she reached the dock, she sprawled on her belly trying to grab me, but I was just out of her reach.

Then, suddenly, she sprang to her feet, cupped her hands around her mouth, and said, "Kevin, listen to me. Just stand up. It's not that deep, honey. Get your feet under you and stand up, boy!"

Turns out, she was right.

I squirmed in the water, got my legs down, and my feet hit the bottom. I stood up and the water was barely above my waist.

If my grandma hadn't come running, I might still be out there, terrified and treading water, totally unaware that my fear was far greater than the depth of my problem.

My heart warmed a bit with memories of those simpler times as a seven-year-old boy. This story serves as a reminder that there are times when we just need to take a stand and rise above our fears and our past. You and I have the power to overcome our challenges, whether in work or in life.

As my grandma taught me, when we dare to stand tall, we often discover our challenges are not as great as the fear surrounding them.

Your Master of Disaster

That fish tale is a true story, a real-life parable. All of the stories in this book are drawn from my life and the lives of those I've known. For better or worse, I have a vast collection of stories, some good and some bad. Many I've never shared in my talks around the world.

You may have heard one of my speeches delivered to a wide range of corporate clients, conventions, and groups. Speaking is my second career, which grew out of my previous position as a corporate marketing executive.

I am not a natural extrovert, by any means. My boss had to push me out in front of my first audiences. Looking back, I think it was entirely appropriate that my first speaking engagements were for a company that specialized in disaster recovery and restoration.

Before I joined what would become a multibillion-dollar company and rose to an executive leadership position, my life had been pretty much a disaster. I might never have recovered and restored it on my own had not my bosses and other heroes shown up to support and encourage me.

My story is about recovery and restoration for those of us who somehow fell off track or screwed up royally somewhere along the way. Maybe you have been in the same situation, or maybe you simply are still looking for a bigger opportunity, a better quality of life, or a more fulfilling existence.

I can help you with all of the above, I believe. Not because I consider myself a self-help guru or a life coach or any of that. I come from a blue-collar background. I have been homeless more than once, living in my car or mooching off friends and family.

My story is filled with lessons that changed me in profound ways. Lessons that continue to forge the steely and stubborn parts of me that apparently needed extra time in the fire. In my teens and early twenties, there were many times when I was in over my depth. I couldn't seem to catch a break or my breath. Unable to stand up on my own.

The lessons and examples I offer in these pages are from my own hard-earned, and gritty experiences. And I use *gritty* because I don't want to hit you with the other __itty word that might be more accurate.

This isn't about some generic system with ten or twelve or twenty-seven steps to success. This is about what worked for me in turning my life around. It's about making changes to become a better person so I could build the better life I so desperately wanted.

I will not give you a list of things to do. The truth is most of us already know what we need to do more of, and less of. The question is, "Why aren't you doing what you know needs to be done?"

It is my belief that people don't fail in life because they don't know what to do. People fail in life because they don't know *how to be*. Once you understand who you need to become, the *how* will reveal itself to you, as it did for me.

I will introduce you to some of the leaders and mentors who helped me turn my life around personally and professionally. These heroes saved me. In sharing my own story of recovery, restoration, and resilience, my hope is that you will learn from my mistakes, as well as from the few successful personal and professional moves I've made in my fifty-some years.

Roughly half of those years were a struggle. I will explain more later, but because of a horrific experience, I quit high school and ran away from home. I was homeless off and on through the rest of my teen years and even into my twenties.

I was lost. I made terrible decisions, hung out with bad people, and to put it concisely, I went the wrong way for a long way.

Strangely enough, I did not begin to turn my life around until I landed a job with a leading disaster recovery and restoration company. I was newly remarried with an infant son. Up to that point, I'd had a hardscrabble life scarred by experiences that I would not wish on anyone.

Marrying Lisa, a beautiful, smart, patient—and apparently extremely near-sighted—woman marked the beginning of a remarkable turnaround in my life. Around the same time, I became blessed by a support team of men and women who showed up at key moments to help me transform my life for the better.

For the *way, way, way, WAY* better.

One of my goals with this book is to encourage you by offering you hope. If you are struggling, in a rut, and desperate to break self-destructive patterns, I am here to tell you that it is possible to do just that.

Too often, we go through life accepting a storyline written by others. But we have the power to write our own stories. I was slow to get that. I spent too many years accepting life as it came instead of creating the life I wanted. Think about the storyline you've been living out. Did you write that story? Or was it written by someone else?

Critics and controllers will try to do that for their own selfish reasons. But you have the power to reject their lies and write your own story.

I encourage you throughout this book to take the pen firmly in hand. Envision the life you want, and create it. Not just on paper, in reality. You have that power. It is yours for the taking.

Take charge of your life, but listen to those who have your best interests in mind. My life began to turn around when positive, but often demanding, people stepped up, put a hand on my shoulder, and said, "No, not that way, Kevin; *this way.*"

Muskegon, Michigan

To help you understand my journey, and why I might have something to say that could help you on your own path, I want to share a little of my background. Not too much, just a little, because as you will discover a little of my history is usually more than enough for most people.

Including me!

I grew up in a Rust Belt blue-collar home. My father was a Navy man, a ship's cook with Popeye forearms and a strong back bent from heavy burdens.

I tried not to add to them, but failed miserably.

When I was born, my dad was in his tenth year of service and stationed in Long Beach, California. Upon my arrival, he abandoned ship, honorably, and we moved to Muskegon where he took a job in a piston ring factory.

It sounds like the setup for a Bruce Springsteen song, I know.

My mom stayed home and took care of me and my older brother, and our sister who came along later. Mom was an unhappy person. She struggled with health problems that were both real and imagined. She wrestled with anxiety and depression. Some said she was a hypochondriac. She self-diagnosed and self-medicated, often demanding treatments and operations that her doctors insisted she didn't need.

Mom had demons that haunted her. She wasn't unloving or uncaring, but she was often unavailable. As a parent, she called in sick, a lot.

As a result, my dad came home from work to even more work. He did his best to be both father and mother, but mostly he was worn out.

Now, after sharing all that, I have to tell you that I was a pretty happy-go-lucky kid throughout my grade-school years. I got high marks, did well in sports, and had a lot of friends. Too many friends, in fact.

Girls wanted only to be my friend, which I found frustrating. The joke was that I had bruises all over my body from being touched with ten-foot poles.

So I had an ordinary childhood until I hit my teen years and moved on to high school. Early in my sophomore year, my entire school was shaken with the news that a smart, athletic, and popular classmate had disappeared.

He'd seemed to have everything going for him, but then he vanished from the classrooms, hallways, and athletic fields.

Rumors flew.

Had he died?

Moved away?

Become addicted to drugs?

Joined a hippie cult?

After a while, everyone stopped talking about him. They went on with their teen years and pretty much forgot that guy.

Me.

I disappeared from that "normal" life. I ran from it. Out of fear, and shame.

Only a few classmates would ever learn the secret behind my disappearance. You see, my dreams of an extraordinary life were dashed by a betrayal most vile.

A trusted adult. A close friend of our family. A hunting and camping buddy. A fellow church member. A man's man with a beautiful wife and a monstrous side.

He groomed me, among many others. Then he shattered my life and crushed my spirit over a period of three years until, broken, tired and scared, I ran.

Late one night, I stuffed everything I had into my dad's old green Navy duffel bag, and there was still plenty of room for all those things I didn't have. The next morning, I left for school but took an entirely different path, and I really never went home again for more than a day or two.

And so began the downward spiral of my lost years. A lost decade, really.

If you've ever had a traumatic experience like this, you know what I'm talking about. Victims often tend to blame themselves, which only compounds the trauma. And when your abuser is much older and more powerful than you . . . well, it can seem that there is nowhere to turn and that the only option is to run from him, run from your guilt, run from the protected and secure life you once thought you had.

If you are in trouble, or know someone in a similar situation, I want you to know that help is always available. You don't have to run. There are professionals who can help you. Call 911. Or if you are too scared to go to law enforcement, then go to a hospital emergency room—even if you are not physically hurt or sick; they will help you and protect you.

Go to the nearest fire department, to your school principal or guidance counselor. They will help you.

You do not have to carry this burden alone. Do not let what happened to you become part of you. Know that you can and will survive this. I survived it, but I wish I'd found help much earlier because I ran from this demon for far, far too long.

The longer you drag those monsters around, the bigger they become. They will seep into every part of your life. They will lurk, hiding, waiting to blindside you when you least expect it. And, unless you deal with them, they will wreak havoc in every relationship. Every time my life began to get better, I would find a way to somehow blow it up.

I was not the only victim to suffer at the hands of this predator. Though we did not know it at the time, there were several of us. This tragedy played out over decades and affected many lives. The predator eventually went to prison, but not for his crimes against us—the statute of limitations had run out on his worst acts—and not for nearly long enough.

One of his known victims became a drug addict and went to prison for eighteen years. Upon his release, he organized some other victims to go public and identify the predator. Before justice could be served, the organizer of the victims relapsed into drugs. One night, he set out to kill the monster, but on the way to the predator's home, he passed out and crashed his car. He went back to prison. Not long after his release, he died in another car crash, leaving a tragic legacy of a stolen life.

You can't hold that amount of guilt and grief and anger inside, because it is like acid that will eat away at you. Help is available. There are experts who can guide you out of the darkness, people who care about you. Do not hold it inside as I did.

Someday I will write about this time in greater depth. Maybe. I will tell you that the valley I entered was deep. I was homeless off and on for years, sleeping in hospital waiting rooms, and using public restrooms. At one point I inherited a family car, a 1975 Ford LTD, which was as big and bulky as a camper, except it lacked a kitchen and bathroom.

Think of it as a *"Fort* LTD."

A few friends and relatives and other good Samaritans took me in now and then, but I usually wore out my welcome in no time. My parents, who had no idea that their predatory friend had targeted their son, tried to reel me back in several times.

They offered their own theories and remedies, and when I didn't get my act together or respond to their demands, they resorted to tough love. I was a truant minor in the eyes of the law, which allowed my parents to send the police after me. They put me in a residential program for troubled kids, Pine Rest Christian Mental Health Services in Grand Rapids.

So, I did what I was best at. I ran.

I managed to squeeze through a secure door before it closed and locked. I ran fast. Faster than I knew I could. There were other kids cheering from the windows high above as I made it "over the wall" and slipped into the thick woods surrounding the complex.

I could hear footsteps behind me. The voices sounded closer and closer. Tree branches whipped my face and arms as I raced through the woods. My feet were cold and damp from running in the soggy marsh alongside a creek bed.

I had no idea where I was going as darkness descended.

I was sixteen and on the run, a fugitive from a prison for messed up kids. My parents sent me there to get help. I didn't want help. As far as I was concerned, I didn't need any help.

Why, then, was I so scared?

I emerged from the woods after more than two hours of panicked wandering. I had managed to elude my pursuers.

I found a grocery store with a payphone just outside the entrance. I called my girlfriend, collect. She didn't take the call. I tried my best friend, no answer. My uncle was my last lifeline. He came through. After promising to pick me up, he called my weary parents who notified the authorities.

Soon I was returned to confinement in a sterile white room, staring out a window covered in steel wire mesh. Lockdown for a week. No visitors and no outside activities. I was a flight risk.

My anger simmered. I was determined to get out of there.

After a week I was allowed to rejoin the other kids, gradually integrated into their activities and therapy sessions. I made some friends. I pretended to do the work.

I figured if I was a good boy and "changed" my ways, they would set me free sooner. Or I would find another opportunity to break free and run.

Running was mostly what I did during those lost years. I was running from a monster and the demons he'd implanted in my brain. I became a different person, driven by fear instead of hope. Or maybe you could say I split into two distinct identities—the Victim and the Striver—which is not at all unusual for someone who has undergone a traumatic event at a young age.

I found I could be who I needed to be to get through each day. I lied to myself and people around me, not so much to be deceitful or to gain any advantage but to bury my secrets and the paralyzing shame within them.

I didn't want anyone to know I'd been abused or that I didn't have a high school diploma or any college credits. You could get away with it back then, before the internet. I learned to package myself well enough as a Striver to get hired for spirit-draining door-to-door sales jobs.

I worked on commission selling encyclopedias, carpet cleaners, and vacuum cleaners. I had a minor victory when I sold a Rainbow vacuum cleaner to my grandmother, but she kept it for the three-day free trial and then cancelled her order on me.

Yep, Grandma outplayed the pitchman!

And that wasn't even my worst experience as a door-to-door vacuum cleaner salesman. Later, while I was pitching my Rainbows, I was driving through a not-so-good neighborhood when my car ran out of gas. This violated one of my father's rules of the road: never let your tank get below half full.

I called a friend to come help me. The friend never showed.

So I walked to a gas station and filled up a gas can.

While I was doing that, someone broke into my car and stole the two Rainbow vacuum cleaners I'd been trying to sell. When I called my boss to report the theft, he didn't believe me.

"I think you sold those Rainbows for cash and made up this story so you could keep the money yourself!" he said.

"You're fired!" he added.

That's how things go when your life is on a downward spiral. I told the truth and my boss refused to believe me. Another job lost in a growing list of missed opportunities.

Somehow, there was enough of the good churchy kid in me, the honest guy, the pleaser, that I didn't get into abusing drugs or alcohol or any of the other sure paths to self-destruction. But the Striver was constantly being dragged down or sabotaged by the Victim.

For the longest time I couldn't hold down a job, so I often had to beg for money from family and friends. I'd even ask my bosses for advances against commissions. I ate mostly at cheap buffet restaurants where I would gorge on food until I could hardly walk, then I'd stuff my pockets with fried chicken, dinner rolls, bread, jelly packets, and biscuits.

I tried to figure out how to steal gravy, too, but it left really bad-looking stains on my pants.

"What's that runny brown stuff on your work pants, Kevin?"

"Uh, just some gravy from dinner last night."

Life in the loser lane was just exhausting. Every day I was fighting for survival. I might have given up all hope of outrunning the demons of guilt and self-hatred if I hadn't discovered a strange cassette tape among the Foreigner, Journey, and other classic rock tapes I'd thrown into the duffel bag.

The title on the cassette said *The Strangest Secret* and featured a photograph of a very straight-arrow guy who looked like a school principal: Earl Nightingale.

I thought maybe it was an old-school jazz tape when I popped it into the portable Panasonic cassette player I pulled from the duffel bag. Then, this big booming voice rattled the windows and began lecturing me about what I was doing wrong with my life, hitting every one of my buttons. Except maybe the part when he said: "You become what you think about all day long!"

My first thought upon hearing that was, "If he's right, I would have turned into Farrah Fawcett by now."

Earl Nightingale was a pioneer in motivational audio tapes, who took author Napoleon Hill's *Think and Grow Rich* self-determination philosophy and ran with it to the recording booth.

I didn't know it when I popped in the first of his tapes, but Nightingale was cast as a hero both in real life and as a radio actor. He was one of the few US Marines on the battleship USS *Arizona* to survive the Pearl Harbor bombings, and he'd been a broadcast star as the voice of Sky King in that early radio series.

Earl Nightingale was the first of many motivational and inspirational speakers to help me see that what had happened to me in the past did not have to control my future. I learned that I could determine my own path, but only if I could summon the strength to fight off the demons.

It took a long time for me to fully grasp the power of that message, of course.

Sitting in the car, listening to his motivational tapes, I was inspired to change my life, but I didn't know how.

I would later learn that the *who* is more important than the *how*.

At that point, I didn't grasp that it wasn't enough to hear Nightingale's message. I had to actually apply it, successfully, consistently, and repeatedly. For a long time, the only thing I did successfully, consistently, and repeatedly was screw up. I didn't think and grow rich. I thought my way into the ditch.

Dysfunction

I took dead-end jobs selling waterbeds, cemetery plots, and health magazines to pay the bills. My floundering eventually found me buffing floors and doing janitorial work in a nursing home.

There, I met "an older woman."

Oh, I know what you are thinking and no! She was not a resident of the nursing home. She worked there too, as an aide. She was twenty-two, five years older than me to be exact. I moved in with her because she wouldn't move into my car. She had this strange thing about wanting a bed and a bathroom.

She told me that she loved me, but she was still seeing other guys. It was my first experience in a dysfunctional romantic relationship. Back then it was just weird and kept getting weirder, so I left and moved back in with my parents, who, much to their dismay, had neglected to change the locks.

My dad had told me never to come back, but he let me stay until I could figure things out. Then I met the attractive neighbor who had moved in next door to my parents. Another "older" woman. She was twenty-five. She thought I was older than I actually was, probably because of my striking maturity and sophistication.

She certainly wasn't blinded by my wealth and high social standing, though to impress her, I soon moved up to being a franchise owner, of sorts.

Shortly before I turned eighteen, I begged and pleaded and somehow convinced my poor father to give me $5,000 he didn't have so I could buy into a franchise opportunity offered in a classified ad in *Success* magazine. The opportunity turned out to be a franchise with a well-known personal development organization, which produced books and tapes and leadership programs that its franchisees schlepped around and pitched to business owners as management training and sales motivation tools.

When my dad gave me the check to buy into the franchise operation, he said, "Consider this your inheritance."

So, I promptly blew it.

I had to lie about my age to get the franchise, but I couldn't hide my lack of experience. Business owners must have found me very entertaining, the high school dropout swaggering in to tell them how I could teach, inspire, and motivate their employees to higher levels of performance.

"Sounds cool kid, come back in twenty years when you have some idea of what the heck you are talking about."

I got a lot of that. I was not doing well as CEO of my own company.

My personal life wasn't any better. My business balance sheet wasn't the only thing with a negative net worth. I was still eighteen when I married "the girl next door." You will be surprised to know that I wasn't ready for marriage. I was broke and broken.

I couldn't support myself, much less anyone else. But I thought this marriage might be the fresh start I needed to turn things around.

I was wrong.

Once again, I failed to be who I needed to be for those around me. My new venture was a colossal mess, and I had no idea how to fix any of it.

The crazy trajectory of my life took me to Waco, a Texas town with a name appropriate for my state of mind. I moved there with my new wife after taking a job in the corporate headquarters of the franchise system I had joined the year before.

Don't ask me how one of their worst salesmen "sold" himself and won a headquarters job. Begging was most certainly involved, as I recall. Maybe they felt sorry for me, or they felt guilty because they sold a franchise to me when I was so young. Or maybe they figured it was safer to have me at headquarters instead of wandering the streets hawking their merchandise with such glaring ineptitude.

A Lost Child

There was no doubt that I needed a steady job more than ever before. I was still a lost boy in many ways, but I also had become a father. I was nineteen when our beautiful daughter was born.

She was a joyful light in the gray landscape of my life, but soon she was taken out of it. My wife and I split up shortly after her birth. She realized I was ill-equipped to be a husband and father.

The marriage was over. I had failed them both.

My wife decided to return to Michigan with our daughter. She had no choice. I had less than no money and even less chance of becoming the person they needed me to be.

The commission-only sales job was another disaster in my growing resume of career lowlights. I found myself alone in Waco. I'm sure there is a country song in there somewhere.

I bounced back and forth between Texas and Michigan after we separated. We tried on and off to make the things work, but in the end, we could not salvage the relationship.

We divorced. The marriage was another broken promise. Something else to put on my pile of regret.

Saying goodbye to my daughter was the hardest thing I had ever done. Yet I knew I couldn't take care of her. Nor could I take the chance of this innocent child being jeopardized by the demons that pursued me. Without me, she at least had a chance to grow up in a safe, healthy, and prosperous home.

I remember holding her tiny hand and kissing her on the forehead. My gut ached as the car drove away. I watched until the taillights disappeared. The feelings of loss and despair haunted me throughout the years.

I hated myself. *What had I done? How could I get this low? I don't deserve to live.*

Lonely and depressed, I fell into yet another dysfunctional relationship with a woman in Texas who had three small children. Another relationship destined to crash.

I thought I could save her and those kids and somehow atone for my failed marriage and the loss of my daughter, but I was wrong. Again.

Some called me a loser, and they weren't wrong at that point. I wasn't capable of being a good spouse, friend, or father. I couldn't settle down because I was still running from the darkness within.

As the country song goes, "I'd been down so long, it looked like up to me."

By now, you may be wondering why you bothered to pick up this book. And why I didn't call it *Unleashing Your Inner Loser: How to Completely Mess Up Your Life and Be Miserable in Eight Easy Steps.*

Well, thankfully, I'm no longer quite the mess I was back then. I am a work in progress these days, and the point of sharing my failures and challenges with you is to help you see that no matter how difficult things might get, no matter how big the screwups, there is always hope. I would not call my own experience a hero's journey by any stretch. Back then I felt more like a zero than a hero.

I've read that the male brain goes through a substantial rewiring process throughout the teenage years and even into the mid-twenties. My rewiring process was probably more complicated than most. I needed more than a tune-up. A complete overhaul was required.

Eventually, thanks to some heroic guides, I would find a path out of my personal hell. The journey would take me out of the valley of desperation and on to a life of professional success and empowering personal relationships. It requires work every single day. There's no magic point in the process when your work is done. But the results are worth it.

You can find your way to the life you desire. I am living proof that it is possible. It won't be easy. You will get knocked down. You will mess up on some days. But if you commit to being better today than you were yesterday I promise you can get to a better place.

My hope is that my journey and the lessons learned will help light your path to a life of excellence in all that you do. Maybe yours will even be a heroic life that makes a positive difference in the world. You see, I believe that in our brokenness we can help others find their wholeness.

Finding Purpose

In the hero archetype embraced by intellectuals, academics, novelists, and filmmakers the protagonist is almost always an ordinary person who encounters some sort of hardship, is knocked down, or is forced to flee from something. Then, as countless stories go, the hero has a transcendent experience and begins running *toward* something: a purpose greater than self-interest, a higher cause.

To take it to the comic book level, which was about as literary as I got in my younger years, think of Bruce Wayne. As a boy, he ran from the memories of his parents being murdered. Orphaned, he went through a period of darkness and self-doubt as a young man, but eventually he found his purpose in pursuing the Joker and other forces of evil. When he focused on serving justice, he found a worthy ideal to run toward, a higher purpose.

Could it be that, for those of us who struggle in our lives, salvation comes when we stop running from our own troubles and begin running toward a higher purpose? Perhaps it comes when we stop focusing on our demons and instead reach out to help others? Can we change the direction of our lives by serving others in heroic ways?

Helping others can help us begin to connect the dots and find answers to our own questions. Don't get me wrong. I'm not saying to ignore your problems. You will have work to do, maybe even deep therapy.

I'm simply saying that sometimes we all need a break. You may need a fresh perspective.

You may simply need some time to catch your breath. But I've learned that helping others find clarity in their lives often has helped me in ways I'd never expected.

Here's what your floundering friend discovered: the first step to changing my life for the better was to change focus from myself and my problems to helping someone with needs greater than mine.

And when I did that, well, my own fantastic force of heroes began to appear. Though, I will admit, it sometimes took me awhile to recognize them.

2

RUNNING TOWARD
A PURPOSE

MY SAD STRUGGLE TO GAIN a foothold in life was interrupted two days before Christmas in 1994 when I suddenly was called to a crisis that, for a change, was not of my own doing.

My uncle called to tell me that my parents had been involved in a terrible car crash in Franklin, Kentucky. My dad had been transferred to his company's factory there a few years earlier.

"Your dad's lungs are crushed. He has broken ribs, a broken collar bone, and a broken pelvis," he said before pausing a second or two to gather himself. "And I'm sorry buddy, but your mom didn't make it."

That was a lightning bolt moment. My heart stopped briefly and then began pumping like never before. My demons and my struggles were no longer important. I was in a terrible relationship that was going nowhere at a record pace. Dysfunctional and out of control.

In truth, I needed to get out of that relationship and onto a more positive path. I was twenty-six years old and ten years into my downward spiral. I had nowhere to go but up, and that phone call would become a reason for turning my life around. A crisis can be an excuse for doing nothing or a catalyst for creating change.

My father needed me, and looking back, I needed to break my self-destructive patterns. When life is spiraling out of control, we feel helpless and hopeless. We isolate ourselves in a cave of pain, convinced that we are alone in our suffering.

I'd been trapped in a cycle of despair, struggling to escape my demons and find a path to hope, a route from where I was to where I wanted to be. There seemed to be this gaping chasm between my potential and my reality.

I had no confidence in my ability to find that path because I'd never been on it. I didn't even know what it looked like. But then my parents' accident forced me out of the destructive cycle and, eventually, helped me find my way back to the "good kid" I'd been before the darkness descended.

Back then, I didn't grasp that I could control my response to the terrible thing that had happened to me. I looked for a silver bullet or magic pill that could end my pain and make everything better. What I did not understand is that when you stop looking back and instead move forward on a more positive track, you build momentum. And that attracts people who want to help you on your journey.

When I went to Kentucky to help my father after the car accident, I found that more positive track. I focused on his challenges rather than my own. I was able to catch my breath and gain perspective. My life gained momentum, and one by one, mentors and guides showed up to help me find the better version of myself.

You don't have to wait for life to send you on a more promising path. I realize that now. In fact, I highly recommend that if you feel stuck, beaten down, or lacking purpose, offer to help someone else in need.

Reach out to a neighbor who could use a hand. Or volunteer at a food bank or homeless shelter. I promise that serving others will bring unexpected rewards and perhaps even life-changing relationships.

Out of Tragedy, a New Purpose

A twenty-two-year-old young man who had been drinking had T-boned my parents' car at a four-way stop. The kid was doing seventy in a twenty-five-mile-per-hour speed zone at night with his car's headlights off.

My parents were a block from home when the accident occurred. They found my mom's body with the house keys in her hand.

My dad was in such bad shape with unstable vital signs that they couldn't risk transporting him in bad weather to the best hospital in the region, Vanderbilt Medical Center in Nashville.

They redirected him to a tiny local hospital where he probably would have died except for the unexpected arrival of a true hero. My aunt told me that a renowned pulmonologist just happened to stop at the hospital to ask for directions as my dad arrived in the ER. That doctor volunteered to help stabilize him so they could take him to Vanderbilt by ambulance. I never learned the doctor's name, but I will always be grateful to him.

My dad woke up in the intensive care unit at Vanderbilt. My younger sister and older brother were there with me. Dad didn't look like anyone we knew. He was swollen beyond recognition, wrapped in a web of wires and tubes, bandages and casts.

Dad regained consciousness as we were discussing what to do about him, where we could take him for rehabilitation and recovery. He waved at us and signaled for us to hand him a notepad and pencil since he couldn't speak.

I thought he might write that he was glad we were there.

But instead, he wrote: Mom?

And so, we had to tell him that his wife of thirty-four years was suddenly gone, killed in the same accident that had crushed his body.

Dad was on heavy doses of morphine. He could not seem to process what we told him in that moment. That was confirmed the next time he woke up a few hours later and asked the same question.

And the next time, and the next.

For the rest of the day, every time my father woke up, we had to tell him again and again that his wife was gone at the age of fifty-four.

The following day, we asked the doctor to quit giving him morphine because we needed to talk to Dad about funeral and burial arrangements. I didn't know if he wanted her services and burial in Kentucky, where they had moved years before, or back in Michigan, where they both had spent most of their lives.

When my father finally emerged from the morphine fog, I leaned down and whispered in his ear, "You can't leave me now. I need you."

He reached a hand to my face, looked into my eyes, and nodded that he understood. I was trying to step up and be the man my father needed me to be, but I was still carrying all of the baggage from the previous ten years. I definitely had tested and strained the bonds of parental love over the previous decade, to say the least.

My parents had no idea what had happened to their former "good boy" who had dropped out of school, run away, and only returned when he needed money or a place to stay between bad relationships.

He'd shown so much promise. Why hadn't he finished high school? Why hadn't he gone to college, taken a good job, married, and had a family?

I had not told them what triggered my sudden personality change and led to my untethered life. My abuser had been their good friend. I didn't think they could handle it. I couldn't handle it either. I felt like a pile of crap. I couldn't get my act together.

My mother's death and my father's injuries finally forced me to grow up. My brother and sister were struggling with grief. None of us had any idea what to do. I felt like I had to be strong for everyone. They were counting on me. I had to figure things out. I fought back my urge to run from yet another traumatic situation. This time, I had to face it and deal with it. If not, my father, our rock, would suffer even more.

Called to Speak

My first experience in public speaking was in front of a large gathering in a small town in Kentucky. I was very nervous about getting up there in front of so many people, including many friends and family members. Actually, I was terrified. I'd never thought of myself as a speaker of any kind. I had no idea who I was and had very little control over my life, so what could I possibly have to say that would interest an audience?

But there I was at the podium with sweat staining my dress shirt. Luckily, I had on a sports coat to hide the downpour. My ensemble was topped off with triple-pleated dress pants and notably bad shoes. I could feel the glares of disapproval coming from my mother in the open casket between me and the mourners.

My father was not there. He was still in the hospital on a ventilator. My aunt read Scripture to him there during the service. I'd been selected by my brother and sister to speak for the family. Let's just say, I was not enthusiastic about their choice. I was afraid my grief and guilt would reduce me to tears. I was the wayward child, unworthy of this task. But there was no one else.

As I stood before those gathered in the tiny chapel, I thought, Mom can hear me.

Then my inner life coach said, No, dumbass, she is not here. So talk about your dad.

Finally, my inner cynic chimed in, But your old man might not make it through this if you don't hurry up.

So I talked about our father being one of the strongest people I've ever known. I justified talking about him at my mom's funeral by noting that I was speaking on his behalf, standing where he would have been if able; to honor his wife and our mother.

She had six brothers and sisters and they were all there. I tried to keep my eulogy as positive as I could. I told some family jokes and reminisced about things that had happened over the years. I also talked about the nicknames they had for each other, most of which were not church sanctioned.

I recalled one of the happiest times from my childhood. Memorial Day, 1979. We gathered at my grandmother's house for a picnic following our annual trek to the cemetery to put flowers on graves and attend the VFW tribute and twenty-one-gun salute. I can still hear those gunshots ringing in my ears. I realized that honoring these true heroes was important and sacred.

There was always plenty of food as well as a lot of shenanigans at my grandmother's house. I shared memories of some of the good times when all the family was there. We all laughed about that one particular Memorial Day in which a baseball game broke out between the kids and the adults.

The kids found a plastic bat and ball, so we went across the street to a schoolyard ballfield and began playing a game with all the young cousins. It was late afternoon on a beautiful spring day in Muskegon, where winter seems to last nine to ten months.

We were lost in the game, whooping it up in the early innings when the grown-ups began walking over to watch. All six of my aunts and uncles. Mom came too. She was smiling, which was a rare event.

My uncle Jim informed us that the grown-ups wanted to play. Them against us. We laughed and giggled at the thought of that.

My cousin Gregg said, "You're too old!"

They accepted the challenge and took the field.

The game was mayhem. The kids doubled-up in laughter whenever one of the aunts or uncles tripped over a base, dropped an easy fly, whiffed at the plate, or took a header while trying to run the bases.

The kid cousins team won, though I don't remember the score. It doesn't matter. That was a good day, and I could see that many in the chapel remembered it fondly. It was a good memory to lean on.

I wanted to be a good son in eulogizing my mother even though we didn't have the greatest relationship. My sister was closer to her because they had a special bond. She is three years younger and the only girl, which by default according to the universal laws of children, makes her *special*.

My sister has had many struggles in life. Mostly, physical. But she shares the common threads of depression and anxiety my mother passed down to us all. My mother was there for my sister. They were pals, but Mom wasn't always available to my brother and me because of her real and imagined illnesses; and because of all the medications she took.

Her pills helped numb her to a false reality, her own world that was her truth. She created her own storyline. You can do that to expand your life and find greatness. Or you can use it to shrink into your own demise. There is always a choice.

Back then, I didn't understand that there is power in simple choices. They can have a profound impact on our lives. Note, I referred to "simple choices." Not easy choices. Often, acting upon those choices can be quite difficult.

Even today, there are times when I need to be reminded that the best life is designed in the moments of simple choices and disciplined actions.

We should never complain about what we allow into our lives. My mother chose to shrink her life. She used to say, "You don't know what it's like to be me." I wish I'd been wise enough then to tell her, "Neither do you. Because you've never stepped into the person you were designed to be."

She allowed her illnesses to become her identity. She let tragedy define her, and as if her real health problems weren't enough, she made up some of her own. She wanted to be seen as a tragic figure, so she collected illnesses and then searched for someone to confirm them as real. It was her way of crying out for attention. It was as if she chased sympathy because she mistook it for love.

Sadly, my most common recollection of my family is the scene of my mother on the couch sleeping or complaining while my dad tried to play both parental roles.

My heart ached for her at times because she never seemed to be joyful or even the least bit happy. Sure, she might smile here and have a laugh there, but not enough to say it was often by any stretch.

I remember her being depressed, mostly, and in physical pain for one ailment or another. She seemed to thrive on sympathy. If you made her laugh, she would find a way to turn it into a tear.

Her depression weighed on me. She never seemed to care about me and what I wanted, so I rebelled against her. There were many times my dad backhanded me in my chair at the kitchen table because I talked to my mom in the wrong tone of voice.

If I made her mad, my mother would wait for my father to come home and then tell him about my latest offense, again real or imagined, saying, "He needs to be whipped."

Dad didn't ask for my side of the story. He just took me out and "tanned my hide," as my grandmother used to say. Half the time, he had no idea why. He was just too tired to deal with it, so he did whatever would appease my mother.

Meanwhile, my sister and brother thought of me as the lucky one who got all the breaks in life because I was popular in school, good in sports, and earned good grades. They didn't understand when I ran away as a teenager. I had never told them about the predator. They thought I'd thrown my life away.

I thought the same, but giving the talk at our mother's funeral and then stepping in to take care of dad during his recovery was a first step, at age twenty-six, in reclaiming my life. It forced me to stop and assess myself and my relationships. I realized that the relationship in Waco was beyond repair. It was time to move on, and my father's needs provided that opportunity.

My dad's brother and his wife had agreed to let Dad and I stay with them in Bowling Green, Kentucky, while he recovered. Dad wasn't ready to be moved home or to live on his own. I loved the time we spent living with Uncle Boyd and Aunt Brenda. They were kind to me, despite my reputation as the family's Prodigal Son.

When Dad and I moved in with them, they shepherded me as I found the path to adulthood. I could talk to my uncle about anything. He was good at giving me advice without making me feel stupid or silly for asking. He was a rock for me during that time.

Uncle Boyd worked for the same piston ring manufacturing company as my father. He was on the engineering side. He'd gone to college at night while working in the factory to get a leg up. My dad worked in the foundry as a front line supervisor.

My dad and my uncle were known as stand-up guys who took care of their people at work. They were like that outside the company too. After I'd been taking care of my father a couple weeks, Uncle Boyd could see that I was getting burned out and restless. I was basically dad's nurse and nurse's aide, tending to his every need.

This was pretty much a first experience for me, taking care of someone in need whom I deeply cared about. But it was exhausting. Uncle Boyd would take me out for dinner or a cup of coffee to give me a break while Aunt Brenda watched over Dad.

I felt loved like never before, and safe for the first time in a long, long time. It got to a point at which I dreaded the thought of going back to Waco where I'd felt adrift. I hadn't really ended the bad relationship there, and though I had a great boss and mentor, I knew there were some lonely days ahead.

I had taken a job for another big multifranchise operation in Waco, and after an initial leave of absence, they let me work remotely while I tended to my father. My new boss, David, seemed like a great guy.

Tough, but caring. He was teaching me the art of selling, while slipping in life lessons along the way. He stressed that you had to be an optimist to succeed in sales, and that was a lesson I needed to learn.

I kept in touch with him on the phone during my time in Kentucky, and he was like a lifeline. He was another reason I remember those difficult times with a certain fondness. This marked the first time I had a support team, and it seemed to be growing as I drew closer to my father and his brother too.

I felt something shifting inside me. My perspective was changing. Taking care of my dad helped me realize that I had more capacity for empathy and more ability to serve others than I had ever imagined.

Suddenly, I was focused on helping him rather than ruminating on my own issues. The shift I felt was my old patterns breaking. If I could help my father, I could help myself. I could become a better person simply by shifting my perspective.

I was changing because I had to. But I couldn't do it alone, and I didn't have to, which was another new thing in my life. Supporters were showing up, attracted by my new momentum. These advisers and mentors would help me clarify my "why" and teach me the "how."

I am still amazed at how many people have shown up in my life to help me conquer the past and create a better future. They are heroes who helped me write a better story than the one I had been living.

Over the years I've been asked a lot about mentoring. I am always reminded of something a mentor shared with me a long time ago. He said, "Only take advice from people qualified to give it." In other words, surround yourself with those who have been where you want to go. Don't make the mistake of listening to advice from someone who has never been where you want to go.

• • •

How to Be a Mentor Magnet

Here's what I believe about finding and attracting mentors to your life: sometimes helpful people will just show up of their own accord at the right time to serve as your mentor, but rather than hoping for that to happen you can make yourself a mentor magnet with a few thoughtful moves.

1. **Show first of all that you are willing to do whatever it takes to do your best and become a better version of yourself.**

    Top performers in any field are impressed when they see less-experienced people willing to do the work neces-sary to master the skill sets required for exceptional per-formance. It's not about showing up your competition; it's about showing up and doing the work, and getting better every day. That may mean putting in longer hours, but in the end, that extra effort will pay off.

2. **Identify top performers who are potential mentors and ask them how they reached the top.**

    Show an interest in them, and they will likely show an interest in you. My advice is that you don't formally ask someone to mentor you, at least not until you've developed a good working relationship. Instead, look for a leader in your field who is willing to give you guid-ance informally at first, and gradually build a mentoring relationship from there if the person is willing to serve in that capacity. Remember, you don't have to stick a "mentor" label on the person's forehead. Most mentors consider themselves to be merely friends or helpful colleagues with their mentees. (I think that's a word, isn't it?)

3. **Listen to the person's guidance with the intent to learn and apply it on a daily basis.**

A highly skilled top performer will take the time to serve as your guide only if you demonstrate that you are absorbing lessons and applying them in your work. Be a sponge. Soak up their wisdom. Ask questions. Take copious notes. No one wants to waste time with a less-experienced person who doesn't listen and learn.

4. **Be grateful and express it.**

Show your gratitude but don't be a suck up. You don't have to win them over with gifts. The greatest gift you can give mentors is to apply their wisdom and better your life. Share stories of how their guidance helped you in your work. Always be careful to respect their time by letting them come to you on their own schedule and at their own inclination.

5. **Adopt a beginner's mindset.**

In other words, be humble and open to advice, information, and direction. You may think you know a lot already, but a potential mentor won't be attracted by a know-it-all. Mentors are drawn to those who show promise and are open to improving their skills and deepening their knowledge.

No one succeeds in life without help along the way. I heard a wonderful story about Muhammad Ali being taught this lesson on board a commercial flight. When the plane ran into some turbulence, a flight attendant came by and noticed the champ wasn't wearing his seat belt.

She leaned down and said, "Mr. Ali, due to the turbulence I need you to put your seat belt on."

Ali looked up, smiled and said, "Superman doesn't need a seat belt!"

The flight attendant chuckled and said, "Superman doesn't need an airplane either!"

We all need help getting where we want to go. We need trusted friends who will support us in our work and in our relationships. I encourage you to remember that as you pursue your own dreams and goals. Look for mentors and others who have a greater perspective, a wealth of experience, and gifts that complement your own. They will help to keep you flying.

Look for Mentors and They Will Find You

I had no idea what a mentor was when David took me under his wing. My first reaction was that he was just being my boss, doing what bosses do, trying to make me a better salesperson so I could produce more profits for the company. Now, that was all true, of course, but it took me a long time to understand that David didn't just want me to be a better salesman. He wanted me to be a better person by investing in my potential. Your mentors and leaders should want to do the same for you.

Because of past bad experiences, I didn't trust anyone who seemed to take a special interest in me. That was a self-defeating attitude, and it took me a long time to trust David so that he could fully mentor me. I am so grateful that eventually he broke through all of my defenses and cynicism and anger to reach into my heart.

Lesson learned: trust people until they prove untrustworthy. Welcome mentors into your life, and let them know you appreciate them as heroes.

After I left the company where David and I worked and joined the restoration company, I met a guy named Scotty, who was a little lost, cynical, and defensive, like I'd been.

I was growing as a leader and I wanted to help others. I tried to do for him what David had done for me.

But Scotty didn't get it.

"I appreciate what you say to me in our meetings and in your speeches to the company, but I don't believe in that stuff much," he said. "You talk about mentoring people, but I've never had a mentor in my life. I haven't been lucky like you were with your friend David. No one has taken that sort of interest in helping me like he helped you."

I couldn't help but laugh.

"Scotty, how long have you been working with me?"

"Three years, why?"

"What do you think I've been doing for you in the last three years? I've been trying to mentor you by encouraging you and giving you guidance. You just haven't recognized it. Your mentors will appear when you look for them. You have to be aware and willing to be mentored."

Potential heroes and mentors are all around you. I learned the hard way that we can become so focused on our problems that we don't see those trying to help us turn our messes into masterpieces.

In my own life, mentors were all around me, but I was so focused on my misery that I couldn't see them. And quite frankly they didn't see me either. They are not attracted to people who wallow in their problems. They are looking for people who are hungry to get over of their problems by getting up off their asses and going to work.

This is a point David often made to me in the early days of our relationship.

"Every time you hit a bump in the road, your wheels come off and you become that angry teenager again," he said. "I can help you grow and succeed, but you have to recognize what I am doing, listen to what I'm saying, and then show up and do the work."

David was not always gentle when mentoring me. Sometimes when I wasn't paying enough attention, he'd have to give my ears a good roasting and my butt a good kicking.

I didn't like it when David chewed me out. In fact, I might have even made it personal. There were times when I didn't like David at all. He demanded that I live up to his expectations. I knew that. I just didn't always know how high his expectations were for me.

You may not always like the people who want to make you better, but being a mentor and a leader is not a popularity contest. When I was a business executive, I wanted people to like me. I hoped they'd like me. But I did not let them slide by or fail to meet my expectations for them.

I wanted them to grow, be their best, and give their best. Whether you are at the gym or on the job, stretching isn't about being comfortable. It is about growing in strength—of body and of character.

I welcomed it when people liked me, but I demanded that they respect themselves. I wanted them to understand that I was trying to help them get better. My job was to remove the barriers to their success. Sometimes, their biggest barriers were themselves.

3

MUTUAL HEALING

DAD AND I LIVED WITH my aunt and uncle for three and a half months, me sleeping on the couch next to his recliner where he was most comfortable. His recovery took six months. It was neither smooth nor complete.

In the first few weeks, my father had terrible nightmares and hallucinations brought on by the trauma and the aftereffects of all of the anesthesia and morphine he'd been given. He'd often wake up spewing gibberish and crazy things.

"Boiled chicken!" was one of his favorite topics in the darkness before dawn.

Dad also had an alarming desire to light and smoke cigarettes while hooked up to an oxygen tank.

"You want to blow us all up?"

The accident severely rattled his brain and altered his personality to a degree. He had always been a funny, quick-witted guy, but he wasn't quite as quick anymore. This was understandable, of course, given all he'd been through.

Yet after six months, he was back on his feet and clear of mind; Dad returned to the factory and worked five more years. Neither my father nor I realized it, but our time together marked the beginning of a transformative period in both of our lives.

My boss, David, had been coaching me on setting goals and then taking steps to achieve them. After ten years of instability, living on the streets at times, surviving paycheck to paycheck, this was an area I desperately needed to work on.

He was always dropping shiny pearls of wisdom on me. One of his favorites: "You gotta have big goals, kid; the kind that require you to stretch and grow in order to achieve 'em."

Helping my father recover provided me with a solid goal. Each day I worked with him helped me realize I could do more and be more. His recovery efforts gave me a purpose, and over time, there were definite rewards for both of us.

His nightmares would wake him up in the middle of the night, and he'd be too hyped up to sleep. Sometimes I'd give in to his request for a cigarette, but only after shutting down his oxygen flow and moving the tank away from his chair. We'd talk about mom and other family members and reminisce some.

One night in the early morning hours, my dad taught me a lesson about forgiveness. Something had been bothering me. The young man who killed my mother and mangled my father in the car crash was being sentenced.

My father requested no jail time in exchange for rehabilitation. My father said if he accepts help and gets clean then that would be the best for everyone. I understood his noble gesture, but it didn't sit well with me. I was angry.

The killer could rot in jail until he arrived in hell as far as I was concerned.

That night I confronted my dad with a question. How can you forgive the piece of garbage who ruined your life?

My dad looked at me and said something I have never forgotten.

"Son, I didn't forgive him for him. I forgave him for me."

I didn't understand. I thought he was talking gibberish again from lack of oxygen.

"What are you talking about?"

"Look, if I carry this around for the rest of my life, it will eat me from the inside out. Hate and unforgiveness can be healed only by grace and understanding. I have to forgive him so I can move on. And I do hope he gets better."

My father then asked me: "Do you want to be held to account for your whole life even though you've changed?"

His words have become a guiding force for me. How can I expect people to extend grace and understanding to me if I withhold it from them?

Powerful wisdom from a ship's cook.

He let me know he appreciated all that I did to help him. We reconnected after a decade of conflict. I began to feel less like a disappointment to him. Then, after three months of helping him, I told Dad it was time for me to return to my job in Waco.

I was not expecting his next move. He handed me a wad of cash he'd had Uncle Boyd take out of his savings account.

"You don't have to pay me," I said. "I wanted to be here for you."

"I know you missed some work to be here, and I'm grateful because I never would have made it without your help. I'm not paying you. I'm just giving you this to thank you and help you out."

I had just turned twenty-seven, but his approval was still very important to me. Years later, I realized that focusing on my father's recuperation had given me a sense of purpose, and his eventual recovery had provided a rare feeling that I'd accomplished something good.

Up to then, I couldn't shake the sense that I was going about life in a half-assed manner, quarter-assed at best. Going through the motions with no idea where I was headed and no motivation to take control of the wheel. I was smoking two packs a day, another indicator of my self-destructive ways.

Whenever I'd get momentum going at work, or in my personal life, I'd sabotage it somehow. I thought the universe was out to get me. But in truth, I was like space junk stuck in a bad orbit, trashing up the universe. That was another thing: I didn't feel worthy of success. I was a high school dropout loser carrying around a dark secret and horrendous memories that came in crippling flashes so painful they were paralyzing at times.

There would come a day when my therapist would help me to see that I was still dragging that angry, ashamed, and scared teenager around. I was afraid my secret would get out and people would look down on me, or worse. On good days, I felt like an imposter. On bad days, I didn't dare to feel anything at all.

When I returned to Waco, I was determined to clean up my life and put the past behind me. I knew David would help me with that, but I had no idea that another coworker would step up and play an even bigger role in my restoration.

4

WONDER WOMAN TO THE RESCUE

THE FIRST THING I DID upon arriving back in Texas was end my latest failed attempt at a relationship. At that point, I had no hope that I would find someone to truly love. Funny how life works out when you open the door to better things.

I first admired Lisa from afar when I went to work for a family-owned Waco company that franchised several service brands offering cleaning services of various sorts.

I was in franchise sales and Lisa was in the accounting department. I chased numbers. She crunched them. She is a beautiful human, so I had noticed her around the office. But we didn't have any contact inside or outside work until we both attended a funeral for the son of a coworker.

The coworker and mutual friend was Leo, who was in charge of the grounds and facilities at our company headquarters. Leo was an old-school Texan. With his salt and pepper hair and bushy beard, he looked like a character out of a Louis L'Amour novel. He was well-liked by everyone at the company; the groundskeeper who kept us all grounded, you might say.

Lisa had become close to him and his entire family, and she was distraught at the funeral of his son, who had been killed. She and I made eye contact at the funeral, and there was a connection for sure.

Lisa had been through a divorce a year earlier, which led to her moving in with a "gal pal" of mine, Jennifer. I finally got to know her while visiting their apartment.

Given my history of relationships with *older* women, you might be surprised to discover that Lisa is three years *younger* than me. I thought I'd try something different, and it worked out very well—once I survived her first home-cooked meal for me, that is.

We hadn't even had a real first date when Lisa said she wanted to make her grandmother's famous fried chicken for me. So I walked two buildings down to her apartment.

As I approached the building, I saw smoke billowing out of their apartment windows. Then I heard the fire alarms going off. I took that as a sign that our dinner plans might have to change.

Luckily, it was all smoke and no real fire. The fried chicken was extra, extra, extra crispy. It wasn't just blackened, it was soot.

Rest assured, no one went hungry that night. We headed to Jim's (not as) Krispy Chicken restaurant down the street. (It was still there last time I checked.)

We had a fine-dining experience of chicken strips and baked beans, then went back to her still smoky place and watched what would become our favorite late-night drama, the cop show *Silk Stalkings*.

(Is that too much information?)

Lisa and I bonded quickly. We'd both grown up in somewhat dysfunctional families. She had met her biological father for the first time just five years before we began dating. The stepfather who had adopted her was not nice to her. She was empathetic about my experiences as a troubled teen, and she has helped me immeasurably with the guilt and struggles over my separation from my daughter.

We became a team dedicated to helping each other face the world and reclaiming control of our lives. We dated just a few months before I went to my favorite exclusive jewelry store, Montgomery Ward, and bought a wedding ring on the installment plan.

It came with a free set of snow tires! (Not true, unfortunately.)

A few days later, I dropped to one knee in her apartment and proposed to her. Despite having good sense in most other situations, she said yes, confirming that she would continue to be a hero in my life, a source of strength, stability, and support.

We were married at the courthouse on our lunch hour. We flaunted all customs and traditions. She had a best man, our work friend Leo, and I had a best woman, Stephanie, who stood up for me.

There were a lot of whispers at work that we'd married too quickly and that it would never last. Twenty-four years later, we're still hoping it works out.

All joking aside (really, just kidding, honey), Lisa took on a lot when she married me. My demons weren't invited to the wedding, but she has had to deal with them over the years. She can always tell when they are dogging me.

"Let them go," she'll say. "Shut out their voices."

I've had professional counseling, which I recommend to anyone burdened by traumatic events, but my wife has helped me through many dark times. I'm sure there are spouses who think they have to fend for themselves and maybe even hide their demons from loved ones.

Sharing my fears was not easy at first, but I'm grateful to have finally found a true partner who is always there for me. On our wedding day, Lisa and I planted a flag in the ground and said, "Go forth and conquer life."

So far, we have persevered.

Lisa has made me a better man and a better person. I tended to be cynical and pessimistic, but she taught me to be more aware and open to the good things in people and in life. She taught me that in every setback there is a seed for something better to come. She believes that everything happens for a reason: the good, the bad, and the unexpected.

She's made me kinder and given me a greater perspective on the world through her positive spirit. She's even had me binge-watching the Kevin Costner series *Yellowstone,* which is my first binge-watching experience.

It hasn't been easy for her. She has endured my failures and frailties, my demons and the darkness. I've struggled with anger. An angry thirteen-year-old boy facing adult problems was not a great combination. And while I've never been physically violent toward another person, I have put my fist through the wall on more than one occasion.

I've harmed myself in moments of rage. For a long time, it didn't take much to set me off. Little things would send me over the edge. There were so many times when I felt helpless and out of control.

When the hot water heater blew up in our first home, I exploded along with it. When the car broke down I did too. And the guy who cut me off in traffic learned everything I knew about sign language.

Honestly, I can't believe Lisa has stayed with me. I've left me so many times I can't count them all. But as my dad used to say, "Wherever you go, there you are."

I struggled to escape my demons. I didn't like myself for many years. Even now, sometimes the demons whisper and I fight mightily to silence them.

I was shocked that someone could love me enough to see through the anger and rage of a broken kid. Lisa, to my lasting gratitude, saw beyond that and recognized a man with some potential.

Lisa has many superpowers. Back then, she instinctively knew that I would need other heroes in my life to help me uncover my potential.

She wasn't shy about enlisting the help of my work mentor, David. She encouraged me to absorb and apply all that David had to offer. And she would go directly to David if she felt I needed a little "extra" mentoring.

Like all heroes, Lisa knows that it takes a team to accomplish great things. Lisa was building our own personal team of superheroes, like the Justice League or the Avengers, to guide us along the way.

A Boss and Mentor

The one coworker who actually thought I had a chance at making my marriage to Lisa work was my boss, David. He was also the main reason I had a shot at making the marriage work—and a shot at finally getting my life out of the decade-long downward spiral.

David was a gruff, no-nonsense sales guy from South Texas who took me under his wing. Maybe he liked lost causes, or big challenges, or wounded humans. He encouraged me, but he didn't put up with any of my crap.

One day I walked into his office and slammed the door behind me. I was seething about my teammates, who were always bickering and complaining when they should have been out making deals.

"They don't get it! All they do is fight and complain about how hard the job is. They can't figure out anything on their own," I said, before losing it completely and screaming: "*I am surrounded by idiots!*"

David's first response was not what I expected.

"Ha!"

I wasn't laughing, so that eliminated any chance that he was laughing *with* me, which meant he was laughing *at* me.

That *really* ticked me off.

I thought I was making a serious point.

My mentor wasn't taking me seriously at all.

"What is so frickin' funny about that?" I demanded.

Cool Hand David took a swig of his coffee and waited for the caffeine to kick in. Then he reached over and turned down the volume on the *Phantom of the Opera* soundtrack that played constantly in his office.

"Son, I have two things for you. You should write them down."

He had a standing order that no one came into his office without a pen and pad of paper so they could write down his David-isms.

I stood with pen poised over paper.

"Number one. You become a product of your environment. It's your choice who you allow to influence you. Just because you work with someone doesn't mean you have to commiserate with them. Wouldn't you rather be the influencer on *your* team?"

"Number two. We reproduce what we are. If you want to be a leader, start practicing how you should lead those around you and build winning teams. You are paid to build our business. You will be respected for building a great life. But you will be remembered only for the people you build."

Class dismissed.

David was not always so patient with me, and that was a good thing. He taught me all that I needed to be successful in sales, and he taught me even more about being successful in life. There is no doubt in my mind that he and Lisa saved me.

I never would have had the courage to marry Lisa if it wasn't for David's belief that somewhere inside my thoroughly messed-up self, there was a glimmer of hope.

When I began working for David, my demons were unrelenting. I still lacked a place to stay the nights, or the days, on more than one occasion. I had not yet shed the victim's mentality.

The hurt, angry, and afraid boy in me would not let the man emerge. I'd have some good months followed by a few bad months and fall back into a scarcity mindset. I was afraid of failing and afraid of succeeding because that scared thirteen-year-old boy didn't believe in himself and didn't trust anyone else to believe in him either.

If I blew a sale or missed a goal and David yanked my chain, I would lash out: "You don't understand. My life hasn't been fair!"

David never let me get away with being a victim.

"Every time your wheels go off the track a little, you want to go back to being a thirteen-year-old," he said. "If you want to stay in that mindset, then you are on your own. If you want to go somewhere new, somewhere better, I can help you, but you have to be a willing participant. You have to do the work and show up."

He'd also hit me with this: "You say you want to go someplace better with your life, but all you talk about is where you've been. Your past is a place of reference, not a place of residence."

Oh, he knew how to push my buttons. There were times when I was so angry at him that I wanted to punch him in the throat. Yet, deep down, I knew he was right, and I knew he was trying to help me become a man.

David did not accept the "poor, pitiful me" lament. He'd glare at me and I'd steel myself for a blast. Instead, in a surprisingly warm and steady tone, he'd set me straight: "Listen to me, son. Life is *completely* fair. Nobody gets out unscathed. You think you are the only one with problems? Guess again."

Then, he'd lay it out for me: "The difference between happiness and misery is as simple as choosing which one you want and then doing the work to make it happen. You can't work on your future while you're stuck in the past."

David held me to a higher standard than I held myself. That's what real friends and mentors do. I've heard people say their closest friends accept them as they are. I believe that people who care the most about you will hold you accountable to becoming the best version of yourself. They do not buy your excuses. They won't let you slide by. They challenge you to do your best and be your best.

Why? Because they know what's in you. They know what you have to offer the world. Heroes hold people accountable to their talents, gifts, and abilities.

Honestly, it's also selfish on their part. They want you to be great. They don't want to miss out on your contribution to the world. Think about that for a minute. What cures, what innovations, what social contribution might never happen if you decide to play small and live an ordinary life?

David poured ideas into my muddled young mind as he rebuilt my confidence and self-esteem. Slowly, the waves of doubt and desperation began to subside. A new sense of calm centered me for the first time since I'd packed that big, green duffel bag and fled my abuser.

He made me aware of the limitations and low expectations I'd set for myself and then challenged me to rise above them: "*If your vision is big enough, the odds don't matter!*" Thanks to David, I was able to step up and support my father after his accident and, in the process, find the path to becoming a better human. He changed the trajectory of my life, really.

His guidance made it possible for me to begin the deepest and most empowering relationship of my life. Having Lisa, my soulmate, and David, my steadfast guide, helped me develop the confidence to end the downward spiral, stabilize, and move up the career ladder further than I ever dreamed possible.

David taught me how to sell, but more importantly, he taught me how to see.

"Selling will help you make a living, but creating a bigger vision will help you build a life," he'd say.

A light came on in my brain. For the first time, I understood the power of running toward something instead of running away from something. I could actually choose my future instead of settling for the present. David always said: "To live in the past is to die in the present, and to die in the present makes the future irrelevant."

David taught me to create a vision for my life, a long-range target to keep me on track. He encouraged me, propped me up when I couldn't stand, and loaned me his confidence when I had none of my own.

That is what true leaders and mentors do. Like David, Lisa doesn't mess around with *what ifs* or even what is probable; she stays in the What Is Possible Zone.

She understands that a compelling vision will draw you in, hook you, and create a path to achieve your goals and dreams. Guided by it, you can find the tools, resources, knowledge, and people you need.

David emphasized the need to create a grand vision, the bigger the better.

"Your goals should be so big that they scare you and make you uncomfortable," he said. "That's the key to becoming the extraordinary person you were meant to be."

He was right. I know. Having a greater vision has lifted me up time and again.

In the past, I had unconsciously set boundaries for myself. I had failed to see that those self-imposed limitations were based on my performance in the past, not on my potential growth in the future. A greater vision will propel you to be larger than your challenges. It will keep you focused on where you want to go.

David opened my eyes so I could see that my boundaries were illusions that I'd accepted as limitations and restrictions.

Years later, I watched a family pet discover this for herself. Her name was Chelsea. She was a bichon-poodle mix. A *bichpoo,* if you must. We lost her in 2020, but we loved her for nearly seventeen years. She was the best dog ever, although we don't say that in front of Buster and Daisy Mae, the current king and queen of Casa Brown.

One of my favorite memories of Chelsea was when we moved into a new but old house in Gallatin, Tennessee. The stately house was situated at the end of a cul-de-sac, and it had a big yard for our little dog to roam.

But there was a problem. Neighborhood restrictions prevented us from putting up a fence to keep our tiny pooch in her own yard. She kept trying to expand her empire, and some of the neighbors were not cool with that.

So after much research and consideration we decided to have an invisible fence installed. Now, I've always had concerns about paying for an invisible fence. I mean, how do you know that you are getting what you paid for?

In fact, Lisa called me on the day of the installation and said, "The invisible-fence people are here."

And I said, "How do you know!?"

Don't feel bad. She didn't laugh either.

They installed underground wires along the perimeter of our property. White flags marked the "inbounds" area for Chelsea's playground.

Next came the training.

Every day for weeks, Lisa walked Chelsea around the perimeter of the property. The idea was to get our dog close enough to the boundaries to see the flags and feel the slight current of electricity transmitted to her new collar.

The collar would also beep if Chelsea ventured too close to the newly established boundaries, so then we'd have a *beeping bichpoo*.

But what man rigs together, nature finds amusing. Our local bird population went to school while Chelsea was being trained. They studied it all, because our dog was their tormentor. If even a sparrow landed on our lawn, Chelsea went on a yapping frenzy.

Have you ever tried eating a worm with a bichpoo roaring down on you? It's not easy, believe me.

Finally, the day came when Lisa believed Chelsea was sufficiently fence aware. On the first day of yard freedom, Chelsea sat on the back porch watching the birds zooming without a care, singing to one another, and obviously taunting her to cross the invisible border and get zapped.

Chelsea couldn't take it. She bolted off the porch and raced at the bold birds. But our ferocious dog was no fool. She stopped just short of the invisible fence. The fowls foiled her. One large bird landed on a stump just across the line and ripped at Chelsea. They don't call 'em mockingbirds for nuttin.'

Still, Chelsea held her ground. No bird was worth a zapping. She knew her limits.

Ah, but then what should appear on the other side but a big fat squirrel? Nothing riled up Chelsea more than a scurrying squirrel.

At first, she sat and observed.

Then she barked and her body twitched.

Finally, she bolted straight through the fence line chasing the squirrel, hell-bent for glory.

She broke through her boundaries. And our dog never looked back. Until dinner time, that is.

Chelsea broke through boundaries imposed on her by others. And if you asked her, she would tell you it was worth every zap!

The path to your best life may require you to break through the invisible boundaries that have held you back. You may get zapped a time or two, but it will be worth the temporary pain to achieve your dreams!

Heroes Are Hopeful

We all have barriers in our life to break through. Some real. Some not. Some we can see and some that are hidden. Hope is something I speak about and share with my coaching clients. It's a concept I call Hopeful Leadership. It shows up in business and in life. It is a critical superpower that heroes and high performers use to create incredible outcomes.

Now, if you're a leader, I know what you're thinking: hope is not a strategy. Right? I hear you. I used to think that too. Not anymore.

Here's what I've learned about the role of hope. The greatest leaders and most heroic people I've ever known deal in a currency called hope. Especially when things are tough. Here's why.

While it is true that hope is not a strategy, no strategy is achievable without hope. Hope is an important piece of a three-part system that the great ones use to achieve high levels in business and in life.

The three parts:

- **VISION**—Big-picture aspiration. This is the main thing. The focus you need to move forward, toward your dreams.
- **HOPE**—This is the inspiration required to get there. The everyday encouragement that says you can do this. This is vision's cheerleader. Why it matters.
- **ACTION**—This is about activation. What do you need to do and whom do you need to become in order for the vision to be realized?

At the end of the documentary *The Last Dance*, which chronicled the remarkable run the Chicago Bulls had leading up to and winning their sixth NBA championship, Michael Jordan said, "It all started with hope."

He didn't say that it started with talent, work, coaching, fans, or anything else. He said it started with hope. Period.

If you want to elevate your leadership and influence personally and professionally, I encourage you to begin bringing hope into the conversation. Hope says you can get there from here.

Hope Heals

You might find it interesting that around the same time I met and fell in love with Lisa, my father was on a similar path. He found and married a wonderful woman who made him the happiest I've ever seen him.

As I write this, he and Jane are still together and celebrating their twenty-fourth anniversary. This is easy for me to remember because Lisa and I married in the same month just a few weeks earlier that year, 1996.

Dad met Jane while he was mowing his backyard. She was visiting her mother next door, and they struck up a conversation over the backyard fence. She brought him a glass of iced tea and quickly won his heart.

Jane has been a powerful force for good, a true hero to my father even as she dealt with major health issues. She is an example of how hope is necessary in everyday life. She has conquered uterine cancer, breast cancer, and liver cancer. As I write this, she is dealing with a diagnosis of Parkinson's disease and a stroke. She celebrated her eighty-first birthday in the hospital. Yet I have never heard her complain. She refuses to be confined by any barriers.

Not once did I hear her whine. No *poor me*. No *why me?* Every day she rises and fights to seize the joy in every moment. She has a vision of good health. She is hopeful. And she takes action.

She also understands the power of humor.

Recently, I asked her how she can keep smiling every day when she is dealing with all she's been through.

In response, Jane unleashed her dazzling smile, pointed at my father and said:

"Because every day I get to be with that hunk of burning love right there!"

Then she added something that floored me. "Listen, son, the doctors can give me a diagnosis and their opinions. But I have a voice when it comes to the prognosis, and I choose hope."

Is it easy? No. But what's the alternative? Quit? Not even an option in her mind. She believes that every morning she opens her eyes is a gift, and she refuses to waste a single moment. She has been a wonderful gift to my father. For the first time in his life, he has a partner who brings him up instead of dragging him down.

Jane has dealt with enormous health challenges that were very real, and she's never let on that she's had a bad day. How we respond to adversity in our lives truly is a matter of choice.

5

DISASTER RECOVERY AND RESTORATION

IN THE SPRING OF 1998, I found myself in Gallatin, Tennessee, boldly applying for a much bigger job with a growing family-owned business called SERVPRO®. This was a great opportunity to work for a leading franchisor of cleanup and restoration specialists, a company poised for exponential growth.

When I interviewed, this business already had around seven hundred franchises and fifty or so corporate employees. I wanted this job for a couple of reasons. First of all, Lisa and I had a three-month-old baby boy, Josh, which motivated me to look for a higher-paying position. Second, we wanted to be closer to my father and Jane, so our son would have grandparents nearby.

My mentor David coached me for my interview because he sincerely supported my new goals for my family. He had always told me: "If you master the art of selling and communicating, you can write your own ticket to success."

I needed all of those skills and more in the series of interviews they set up to see if I was a good fit for their opening. Whoever got this important position would be selling their franchises in the eastern United States.

My first meeting was with Danny, the director of franchise expansion and one of the nicest people I have ever met. We talked a bit, then he gave me a tour of the corporate campus before taking me to lunch at a wonderful greasy spoon diner. For the rest of the day, I smelled like smoked barbecue ribs. Come to think of it, I had to burn that suit or risk being ravaged by a pack of dogs driven mad by my meaty scent.

After lunch, ol' smoky here met with Rick Isaacson, a member of the founding family, and a leader in the company. I was nervous. He was a co-owner. My performance in the job would directly affect him in many ways.

He didn't mess around.

"Why should we hire a thirty-year-old guy without a college degree who has an up-and-down track record?" he asked.

"I can't answer that question. It would be a leap of faith to hire me, certainly, but I would do everything possible to make sure you never regretted bringing me on board."

I explained that I loved helping people become franchise owners, because for many it is the least expensive and most accessible opportunity for hardworking, down-to-earth people to buy into the American dream of owning a business, achieving financial success, and elevating their lives.

I thought it was a good, if brief, interview.

He didn't make any promises, noting that "the decision will come from the executive committee. We are a family business and very careful about who we hire."

Even though Rick hadn't offered me a job, I felt so confident after our interview that I told Lisa, "If they offer me $50,000, you can stay home and be a full-time mom to Josh."

We got a little carried away, to tell you the truth. Lisa and I even went house hunting in Gallatin after the interview. Call us crazy, but we put down our last thousand dollars in savings as a deposit on a townhouse before heading back to our hotel to pack for our return to Texas.

I probably would have had trouble sleeping that night if Danny hadn't called before we left the hotel. He straight up offered me exactly the salary I'd been hoping for—a $50,000 base salary, the most I'd ever been paid in my life. (Later, I found out that it caused a little turmoil with the company because it was the most they'd ever offered an employee coming in at that level.)

Lisa and I were excited beyond measure. We saw this as a life-changing opportunity. In fact, we saw many lives changed for the better. Those who bought franchises with our company were from all walks of life. They wanted to become business owners, which allowed them to take control of their financial futures. This was a profitable business with a noble purpose to serve others.

Disaster cleanup is, by its nature, a dirty business. Nobody wanted to see our trucks in the driveway, that is until the yogurt hits the fan and they had a disaster to deal with. Our service was about restoration for the customers whose homes and lives had been turned upside down.

For the franchise owners, it was about benefitting from their own hard work to get out of debt and prosper. Our motto for them was Changing Family Trees, because owning a franchise helped many of them build·wealth that meant greater financial security for themselves as well as their children and grandchildren.

It's worth noting that in my first year with the company, Danny became one of several team members who left their headquarters jobs to buy their own franchise with the company. I saw that as a great testimony to our business model, which was designed to help aspiring entrepreneurs succeed.

The culture within the company was all about working hard, serving others, and improving the quality of life for the people we served and served with. It was like a big nurturing family. Sometimes we butted heads, but mostly we worked with a common purpose to make life better for everyone involved. Heroes always make life better.

Ted, the company founder, was sitting in the audience during the first training meeting I participated in. I'd done some presentations to small groups, but this was a corporate-level meeting. I hadn't met him yet, and I didn't know he was there.

Even so, I was still fairly new with the company and as nervous as a long-tailed cat in a room full of rocking chairs. I wanted to be professional, so I played it straight in leading my part of the meeting, and apparently, I failed miserably.

Ted walked up to me at the end.

"I'm Ted," he said, extending his hand.

"*The* Ted?"

"Yeah, that's me."

Then he leaned in and quietly said, "Next time, leave them with something to think about. You didn't leave them anything today."

Ted was the ultimate visionary. He came up with the unusual color scheme for his company logo and vans by going door to door with a paint-sample chart. He'd flash the chart, then hide it and ask, "What colors do you remember?"

Green and orange apparently were the most memorable shades in the neighborhoods he targeted. Ted, who died in 2017, was a very creative guy and a natural-born salesman. His franchise owners revered him. They often kept photographs of him in their homes because he helped them accomplish their dreams.

Ted became one of my biggest champions within the company, and his advice that day still inspires me in my second career as a professional speaker. I think of it every time I step in front of an audience or a microphone.

In fact, Ted also was one of those people who encouraged me to speak at our corporate events, though he joked that it was mostly to keep down the costs of our meetings.

"I don't know why we spend money on keynote speakers when we have one of the best working for us already," he'd say.

Before I joined the business, Ted and Doris had sold the company to their sons, Randy and Rick. Together, the two boys along with Rick Forster, a longtime friend of the family and part of the executive team, would begin growing the business. The boys were joined later by their sister, Sue, which put all the pieces in place. The four of them became my mentors and coaches. Under their leadership, I was promoted to executive management. I led the franchise expansion division first and would later take on two more divisions, marketing services and meeting services.

At the time, I was one of only two executives in the organization who weren't family, but they made me feel like part of their family. I learned a great deal from them. They are true entrepreneurs.

I like to think I helped a little in the company's success, and I think they would agree with that. They certainly made a dramatic difference in my life. They challenged me constantly. They did not coddle me at all. Yet I knew that they believed in me and wanted me to succeed.

I helped them and their team increase franchise sales dramatically, and they rewarded me with promotions, pay bumps, and profit-sharing plans. Let me tell you, I was the most grateful son of a gun in the world because for the first time in my life, I was in control of my life, and even better, I could see that I had *a future.*

My enthusiasm only grew when they promoted me to director of franchise expansion upon Danny's recommendation. They put "the kid" in charge of that important division, and I never looked back.

Ted's youngest son, Rick, who is seven years older than me and currently the CEO, became my boss, and like his father, he was always pushing me to be better and do better. I had been an introvert for most of my life up to that point, but bosses "outed" me into becoming more of an extrovert, sometimes in horrifying ways.

Our company wanted to kick off an "Adopt a Franchise" program at our annual convention in 2002. The idea was to pair more experienced franchise owners as mentors for the newer owners. Rick decided that it would be fun to have me introduce the program while dressed up in a baby diaper, holding a bottle, and riding in an oversized stroller.

Now you know what I meant by "horrifying."

I fought him tooth and nail, so to speak. He let me wear shorts instead of a diaper, but that was all the ground he'd give. In fact, he also demanded that I set up the introduction for the keynote speaker for that convention—minus the baby getup—who happened to be one of my favorite motivational authors and speakers, business leadership expert John Maxwell.

Rick's instructions for my fifteen-minute setup were not extensive: "Be funny and don't screw it up."

The leadership guru was sitting in the front row, wearing his usual tan jacket and black mock turtleneck. I remember that because I was wearing the same outfit, as were all the top executives of our company. We were big Maxwell groupies. Maybe even cultists.

So with our inspirational leader sitting right in front of me, I began my introduction talking about how our company had done many seminars, workshops, and programs using Maxwell's books, audio tapes, and videos over the years, and our business had benefitted from his wisdom. Then, remembering my boss's instructions to "be funny," I unleashed what may be one of the lamest jokes in the history of public speaking.

"Yes, John has become such a big influence on our company that we all drink Maxwell House Coffee at the office."

Yes, I said that. (*Shamefully.*)

There were a few scattered courtesy chuckles, and I thought I heard a groan or two. I didn't dare to look down at John Maxwell's reaction, but later he came up to me and said, "I enjoyed that little thing you did."

Faint praise, I know, but I accepted it with gratitude. If I had a tail, it would have been tucked between my legs, wagging slightly.

I thought that would mark the end of my boss pressuring me to take a more visible position within the company, but I was wrong.

"Great job. We need to get you out there more at our events," Rick said.

Like his father, he saw something in me that I did not know existed. He kept pushing me. My natural inclination was to resist. Even today, I have this innate fear of being exposed as a fraud, or as deeply flawed, so there is still a part of me that wants to hide or at least keep a low profile.

But my work family, which included Lisa, and my former boss David, kept encouraging me, and slowly, I began to grasp what they saw in me, even if I had difficulty seeing it myself.

I learned many lessons from mentors in those years. I felt as though I'd arrived in Gallatin with a GED and left with a PhD. The culture was very entrepreneurial, from top management to franchise owners and their employees. The focus was on executing with excellence and being open to new opportunities. No one sat around waiting for a big break.

They believed that "now always leads to next." If you are present and fully engaged in every moment, you will be prepared for opportunities as they arise. But if you are just biding your time day to day, you won't be prepared to make a leap. As a result, you will remain stuck where you are.

I am often asked by friends and family if I wished I had left my executive position sooner to pursue life as a full-time motivational speaker. My answer always surprises them. I tell them that I made the leap at exactly the right time. I was not ready before that. I had to keep working. Contributing. Improving.

Timing is everything, they say. I waited for the right time and the right way to move on. How you choose to leave an organization matters. This organization was my adopted family. It was not easy to leave. But it was time to step into my destiny. I had done the work necessary to hone and polish my speaking and storytelling skills while also establishing my credibility as an executive and leader.

It took nearly twenty years to prepare for my "overnight success." Whether you are in a corporate job or self-employed, I recommend that you always strive to be your best wherever you are in your journey, because opportunities for greater achievement will arrive when you are ready for them. Right now is preparation for what's next. Be a good steward of now, and what happens next will likely blow your mind!

Stepping Out and Stepping Up

At Rick's urging, I began leading more corporate meetings with head-quarters staff and franchisees. Nearly all of them involved PowerPoint presentations, so it wasn't glamorous. Then, in 2008, as we were planning our annual convention with all of our franchise owners and their teams, Rick said, "I want you to be one of our keynote speakers this year."

I stifled the urge to run out of the conference room screaming in terror.

"Oh, really?"

"Yeah, so get with the team and figure out a topic."

"What topic?" I asked meekly.

"I'm sure you will figure it out. Just keep me posted."

"Are you sure you want *me* to talk for an hour?"

"Yes, I want you to speak, but not for an hour, Kevin! Keynote speeches on the main stage are for *seventy-five minutes*! Just do it!"

Suddenly, I felt a little sick.

6

SEARCHING FOR HEROES

I TOLD MY BOSS THAT I'd give some thought to a theme for a keynote speech. He could tell that I was intimidated. So over the next few weeks, he kept calling me to ask how it was going with the speech. Finally, after his third or fourth call, I said, "Rick, do you trust me?"

"Yes, I guess."

"Well, I don't want to do another ordinary PowerPoint presentation or some canned corporate speech, so you have to give me some time and space to figure this out."

"Okay, I trust you, Kevin. Do what you do best. Do you at least know what you plan to talk about?"

I fumbled for an answer. I didn't want to seem unprepared. But my response came out of the blue.

"I'm thinking of talking about heroes."

After what felt like an eternity of silence, Rick said "Perfect! That's exactly what our franchises are to our customers!"

At first all I could think was: Heroes? What the hell do I know about heroes?

When I sat down to think about that topic, I couldn't shake mental images of men in tights leaping off tall buildings, hanging upside down in a cave, or shooting webs from their wrists. I also had much more intriguing visions of Wonder Woman, which I didn't try to shake at all.

A Brief Flight of Fancy

My mind drifted to my childhood experience as a superhero wannabe. I'd go to bed and pray that when I woke up, I'd have X-ray vision and the power of flight. Or the ability to shoot webs from my wrists. (Until I read more comic books, I was not clear on how that worked for Spider-Man. I mean, were their holes in his wrist?)

Adults don't have those "silly" dreams, which is too bad. Somewhere along the way, we become convinced that there's nothing special about us. We are easily lulled into complacency, satisfied with ordinary lives.

I read a news article about window washers dressed as superheroes who cleaned the windows of a local children's hospital. As the heroes descended from the roof, the sick kids would flock to the windows, pressing their tiny faces against the glass, filled with joy and happiness, distracted from their illnesses and struggles.

These window washers were healing heroes to these kids. You see, the difference between those kids and their adult counterparts is that those kids still believed. Most adults lose that ability. Put those same window washers outside an adult hospital and those patients would be pushing the buzzer for security because there's some nut job hanging outside in a Captain America outfit.

I was one of those kids who believed that I could fly. I figured I was destined to be the next Superman, whenever Clark Kent retired. In fact, I used to wonder why Superman ever wanted to be Clark Kent. I mean, if you had all the "superness" in you, why would you ever choose to be ordinary?

As I got older I realized a lot of grown-ups do that.

I wanted to be the man of steel. I thought it was a job that anyone could get. So I spent a lot of time practicing superhero skills. I'd tie a bath towel around my neck and run through the house, jumping off furniture.

It drove my mother crazy. (My wife doesn't like it, either.)

One day I was caped up and feeling extra super, so I climbed the kitchen cabinets next to the refrigerator. I took a deep breath and jumped. I landed on my feet and thought, "Time to fly higher."

I went outside and climbed the tree next to our garage so I could get onto the roof. I walked to the edge with my cape flying dramatically in the wind behind me, remembering the television announcer's words before every *Superman* show, "Able to leap from tall buildings in a single bound."

(I later realized there is no "from" in that sentence.)

I stretched out my arms and leaped in a single bound, whatever a bound was.

Apparently, Mom had washed the flight right out of my bath towel. Super me plunged straight down. I hit the driveway like a sad sack of concrete.

My super genes that made me imperviousness to pain had malfunctioned. My whole body hurt. Enter my mother. She may have been sickly, but when she was angry she could crank up a lot of power. Her arm strength was quite good, in fact.

I know this, because once she determined that I was not seriously injured, Mom gave me one of her classic spanking-while-speaking punishments. You may have experienced these too.

As she delivered slaps to my butt, she also delivered a verbal message in syncopation: I—*whack!*—told—*whack!*—you—*whack!*—never—*whack!* . . .

Yes, I got a good spanking and Not-So-Super-Son was summarily grounded.

(Disclaimer: This story is not meant as an endorsement of child spanking and/or spank-talking in any way, shape, or form. It's just what happened to me and my boy butt back in the day.)

If It's Green and It Glows, Avoid It!

My mind was still stuck on the superheroes of my childhood, including both their strengths and weaknesses. I flashed back to Superman, whose only weakness, aside from women with the initials L. L., was kryptonite. Not to be confused with cryptocurrency, which has brought down many foolhardy investors, kryptonite is the name given to the glowing green asteroid fragments from Superman's home planet, Krypton.

These bits of home that fell to earth when Krypton exploded were altered by the explosion. Whenever Superman came near them, he turned into a super wimp. A mere mortal.

Think about that: How many of us are weakened by fragments from our own pasts? I certainly was. For years, I let something horrible that had happened to me in my childhood cripple my vision for my life. In retrospect, I kind of wish my crippling fragments were green and glowed like kryptonite because at least then they'd been more obvious to me.

Until David and others stepped up in my life, I did not fully understand what was holding me back. What about you? What is stealing your greatness and leaving you helpless, hopeless, or weak? What fragment from your past is keeping you from your best life?

Now you may say that hurtful and mean people—or hurtful events—have held you down, but we all encounter nasty people, and there aren't many who haven't been slapped down by life at one time or another.

All the successful people I've known can list the critics and enemies who tried to stop them, and all of the horrible setbacks that they had to overcome to be successful. So you can't blame outside forces.

You have to look within. That's where your superpowers of self-determination and self-motivation dwell. What can you do to get up, up, and away?

Well, whenever Superman was brought down by a kryptonite rock, he crawled and clawed to get away from it.

Okay, granted, Superman is fictional. Kryptonite is not real. But neither are most of the things limiting your life. As long as you believe in yourself and refuse to give up, you can overcome any hurtful fragments from your past, any criticism, any treachery, any failures or calamities.

Whatever the kryptonite is in your life, you must do everything within your power to rise up and fight to fulfill your greatest potential. Let me suggest a first step: Rise up and move toward your most compelling vision. Use your "superness" in service to others, and you will find strength to continue your own journey.

Super Search

I tried to get back on track and focus on the speech, but then I saw an ad for *Superhero Movie*, which I'd been hearing about. Made by creators of *Airplane!*, it was a spoof of the endless number of films from this genre including all of the Batman, Superman, Spider-Man, X-Men, and Wonder Woman movies.

I decided my boss wasn't looking for a spoof. He wasn't the spoofing kind.

Yet once the word *hero* was on my mind, it jumped out at me from the strangest places. Even more recently while working on this book,

I stumbled across a magazine article with the headline "Jose Cuervo's Sales Prove Tequila Is the Hero of the Lockdown."

Seriously? A brand of tequila? Is it also the hero of the hangover?

My dictionary reported that *hero* traces back to the ancient Greek term for "protector." Back in those days, Hercules was a hero. In more modern times we think of world changers like Nelson Mandela, Martin Luther King Jr., and Mother Teresa as heroes.

Then again, sports figures are often tagged as heroes even though they are just playing games. While reading the sports section in newspaper, my eyes hit upon this line: "Mookie Betts won free tacos for everyone for a second time and instantly became a hero."

What? Turns out the Dodgers right fielder stole second base during a "Steal a Base, Steal a Taco" promotion by Taco Bell and thus performed an act of heroism.

I like Mookie, but come on, people!

I began to stress that the whole hero thing was being devalued, but then one night Lisa called me her hero for helping with the dishes, and I felt pretty darn special.

(She may deny that happened, but this is *my* book, darn it.)

I began to think that our culture might be approaching hero overload at heroic proportions. Even when someone does something that is truly heroic, they tend to say, "I'm *not* a hero when I pulled that family out of their burning car. My instincts just kicked in."

My research for the speech was going nowhere.

Then I remembered something I'd heard from our advertising firm.

"We are getting feedback from our insurance partners and customers who say our franchisees and employees are heroes for helping them recover from disasters."

I liked that! What if I focused the speech on ways in which everyday people can use their special talents, gifts, and knowledge to serve others in extraordinary ways? That's heroic stuff, right?

I remembered that our advertising company had worked on developing that storyline about heroes by collecting stories from customers and employees around the country. My research led me to a wonderful example of an employee who rose above and beyond to provide exceptional service to an eighty-seven-year-old customer named Mrs. Johnston.

Her insurance agency had called in one of our franchisees after a fire had ravaged most of her home. When our guys walked through the heavily damaged home to make their assessment, Mrs. Johnson tearfully talked about wanting to get her home and her life back.

Our man on the scene, Richard, is not a licensed grief counselor, but he did his best.

"We will fix all of this and your house will be better than new," he said. "I promise you Mrs. Johnston."

He spoke encouragement and hope to her, which was not part of his job, but it was part of his character.

They made several passes through the house to make sure they noted everything that needed to be done. Richard noticed that every time they passed a spare bedroom, Mrs. Johnston would pause, look in, and shake her head in sadness. Sometimes, she would hold her head in her hands as she stood in front of that room.

Finally, Richard said, "What is it about this room that makes you especially sad, Mrs. Johnston?"

She walked him into the room and pointed to a charred piano bench in one corner.

"My grandfather made that for me so I could take piano lessons when I was eight years old," she said, wiping back her tears. "I learned to play on that bench. It has always been important to me."

"Would you mind if I take this to my shop and see if we can fix it? We'll see what we can do with it, Mrs. Johnston," said Richard.

Richard was known for his skills as a woodworker. He took the old, charred piano bench to his work shop and went to work on it. He took the hardware off and worked on that. He sanded it, added wood paste, and after many hours, he brought that bench back to its original condition, a memory made new.

Then, a few weeks later, he brought it back to Mrs. Johnston in her fully restored home. He'd wrapped the bench up in white packing paper, so she opened it up like a Christmas gift.

She'd found it on her kitchen table and opened it like a child on Christmas morning. When she saw what he'd done, she lit up like she was eight years old again and seeing that piano bench for the first time.

"Oh, thank you, thank you, thank you!"

This time, her tears were not sad. They were joyful.

Richard shed a few happy tears himself that day.

Then, two weeks later, Mrs. Johnston's son called to say that she had passed away.

"I wanted to tell you that my mom was grieving terribly after going through that fire, but your crew really helped her have hope again. And when Richard came back with that piano bench completely restored, well, I think it was the happiest I've seen her in many years. You have no idea what you did for her. You brought peace to her life after she'd gone through a horrible time. You really made her final weeks so much better. She described you as her hero."

For many years after that, Mrs. Johnston's son called that franchise office on her birthday to thank Richard again, which was a big point of pride for all of our franchises and their employees.

This story helped everyone in the company see themselves serving as heroes to our customers in their time of need, and it had a powerful impact throughout our headquarters and franchises.

We all have the capacity to do extraordinary things. We can't all fly, or leap tall buildings in a single bound, but we can choose to make the most of our God-given talents to serve a higher purpose.

Find your own "piano bench opportunities." Serve every Mrs. Johnston you meet by putting your brand of excellence to work. Success isn't really that complicated. Do your best. Be your best. Make life better for others. *That's it!*

Naturally Selected for Greatness

Early in my research of heroes for my speeches and this book, I relied on a common definition of what it means to be a hero: "Ordinary people who do extraordinary things."

I liked that at first; after all that's how we've been conditioned to think about heroes. But that doesn't make it right. As time went on I began to wonder, "Is that really true?"

Are heroes really just ordinary people doing extraordinary things, or is there something more to it? Something I missed. The more I looked at this, the more I began to think that no one is born to be ordinary. Are they?

(Metaphor alert: please bear with me!)

Think about it: the day you were conceived, a miracle occurred. Science tells us that when you were dropped off at the pool, there were around a hundred million other kids dropped off that same day—one hundred million applicants for the job of being you. And only you got through.

You went to work, paddling your way through the crowd. Out of the shallow end and into the wide-open ocean of pure possibility. Wearing your tiny cap and goggles, you started moving, and all of a sudden, you hit your stride.

Like a little Olympian swimming for gold, you crossed the finish line first. You made it through. You beat the odds. You became the miracle. And nine months later, you received your gold medal: the gift of life! Your own heroic story to write.

Face it, you were born to be an exceptional human being. You were a miracle at birth, endowed with the talents, gifts, and abilities that are as unique as your fingerprints. There's nothing ordinary about that in my book.

Being *ordinary* is a choice, and not your best option. It suppresses greatness and fosters a false sense of comfort and security that can result in a life of mediocrity. To live a heroic life, you reject being ordinary and do everything you can to exceed expectations and break through barriers.

The truth is, heroes are extraordinary people who choose not to be ordinary.

Every day heroes show up with their best stuff when it matters the most. They choose not to settle for anything less. They are willing to do the hard work, putting in the time, effort, and mental focus to bring forth their "superpower" gifts.

What are our superpower gifts? Well, I don't know about you, but I consider anyone who can take the engine out of a car, repair it, and put it back in to have superpowers. Or someone who can paint a beautiful portrait. Or build a house. I mean, the plumbing alone would be beyond anything I could dream of doing. I break down in tears trying to fix a leaky pipe under the sink. Plumbers have superpowers, right?

Anyone who makes difficult things seem easy—anyone who has worked to master a craft in order to serve others—each of them has the hallmark of a hero.

Unfortunately, far too many people don't develop their gifts to the fullest. They don't put in the extra effort to rise above and beyond. They stunt their growth by letting their unique abilities and gifts go to waste. Maybe they tried once and didn't get quick results so they gave up.

What if Michael Jordan had quit trying out for his high school basketball team because he didn't make the varsity squad his sophomore year? What if prima ballerina Misty Copeland had quit the American Ballet Theatre at eighteen when a fractured vertebrae forced her to wear a brace and stop dancing for a year?

Too many people give up too early in the game. They settle for small lives instead of striving to fulfill their extraordinary destinies. They cling to a comfort zone instead of pushing to break through.

Now is the time to unleash the hero within you. I challenge you to begin pouring your gifts into the world and raise the bar on your capacity. What are you waiting for? Permission? I'm giving you permission right now to step into your best life.

But don't thank me. I'm doing it for me and the people I love. I'm being selfish. I don't want to miss out on the inventions and innovations that are within you. If you choose to live your life in Smallville, you are intentionally denying the planet of your superness. (Yes, that's a word.)

Here is what I have discovered: it takes just as much work to be a small, ordinary version of yourself as it does to be the exceptional person you were born to be. Do yourself and the world a favor and choose to rise above the ordinary version of yourself. Don't settle for less than your best.

More Grounded, in Reality

When it comes to heroes most people would agree that the conversation begins by honoring the brave men and women in our nation's armed forces and those who put their own lives on the line while serving as first responders to emergencies and disasters.

First responders and those who defend our liberty are the gold standard as true-life everyday heroes. I have a friend who is especially avid about honoring and appreciating those in the military. Sometimes, she can be a little over the top in that regard.

Her name is Lisa, but this Lisa is not *my* Lisa. This *other* Lisa is the wife of my best friend, Chad. (We hang out a lot because it's easy for us to remember the names of each other's wives.)

Chad's Lisa is the most patriotic person I have known. When she sees men or women in uniform, she makes a point to thank them, hug them, and exalt them. If she sees them in a bar, she buys them a drink. If she sees them in a restaurant, she buys them a meal.

(If you are in the military, send me your cell number. I will call you if I ever hear Lisa is at a Mercedes dealership! You never know, she is very generous.)

Seriously, Lisa's appreciation for members of the armed forces knows no bounds. I witnessed this again when the four of us made our regular Friday visit to our favorite gourmet restaurant.

We'd just picked up our Cracker Barrel menus when the hostess seated a guy wearing fatigues right next to us. He was alone and looked weary.

I grinned at Chad.

Chad winked at me.

We knew Lisa the Patriot was about to spring into action.

Sure enough, before I could decide between the chicken pot pie or the meat loaf, Chad's Lisa was on the move. She made her way over to the poor guy's table and plopped down across from him, flashing her winning smile.

He was totally surprised and, since he'd seen Chad at our table, not sure what the heck she was up to.

"Ma'am? Can I help you?" he said, warily.

Liberty Lisa reached across the table, grabbed his hands, and pulled him close.

"Sir, I just want to thank you for your service to our country. I want to thank you for working every day to keep our country safe and free. I have two boys, two dogs, and a husband, Chad. Thank you for keeping us all safe."

When Lisa of the USA thanks soldiers, she always uses that same order. First her sons, then her dogs, and finally Chad.

The guy in fatigues blinked a couple times, tried to talk and couldn't.

Chad's Lisa has that impact on people.

In fact, she was about to unleash her favorite shock and awe move.

"Sir, it would be my honor to buy your meal as a small token of appreciation for all that you do for our nation and its people."

At that, the guy let out a loud laugh and then flashed a sheepish grin.

"Aw, shucks, ma'am. I'm not in the military. I've just been out hunting!"

Red, White and Blue Lisa turned entirely red as she retreated to our table of cackling crows hiding behind our menus and trying not to disrupt the Cracker Barrel crowd.

Just when I'd get control again, Chad would lose it, and then we'd start roaring together. The dynamic Lisa duo shot us tandem looks of disapproval indicating that there would be no more fun that night if their husbands did not rein it in.

Chad was no fool.

He stepped up to the plate and knocked one out of the ballpark.

"Baby, you can never go wrong doing the right thing. I'm proud of you, and we are definitely buying that man's dinner!"

There are worse things than buying a hungry hunter's dinner, right? In fact, if you're ever headed to a Cracker Barrel on a Friday night, you might want to throw on some hunting gear.

If the right Lisa is in the house, you could be in luck.

Chad nailed it. Too many people see life as an opportunity for transactions rather than for transformations. I think it is far better to think like his Lisa. She wasn't looking for a payoff. She was simply moved to express gratitude by making a small payout.

Still, her case of mistaken identity got me to thinking: "Is there a surefire way to identify everyday heroes?"

Heroes in the Mirror

I wrestled with that question while preparing my speech. So I did what all smart men do when they need inspiration: I went to my inner circle of wise and worldly advisors.

In my case, this meant my wife.

When I married my own personal Lisa more than twenty years ago, I married up, way up. She is gorgeous on the outside and equally as beautiful on the inside. She is the most positive person I know, and I love her more than anything else on the planet.

She's also very good at stirring my creative juices, so I explained that I was having speechwriter's block—if that's a thing—with the hero speech I recklessly had promised Rick I would deliver for our annual convention.

Lisa has a loving way of calming me and getting me to focus on the task at hand. She could tell that I was nervous. She sat down, took me by the hands, and said that I should just go up on the stage and tell them my own story.

"After all, everyone can learn from your failures, poor decisions, and bad judgment," she said. "Besides, people will feel better about their own lives once they've heard about yours."

Her words made me chuckle. And then I thought, "I still love her, but Lisa is no longer part of my inner circle."

Not really. I kept her in the inner circle. I hate sleeping alone.

But I wasn't sure my story was on topic for this speech.

"Help me understand. I'm supposed to talk about heroes, so what does that have to do with my life?"

Lisa gave me one of those men-are-so-dense looks, let out a sigh, and said, "Let me explain it this way: when you look in the mirror every day, you are looking at the product of all the heroes in your life."

I nodded, pretending to understand. I do that a lot.

She saw through that and continued: "We are all the result and the accumulation of the people who've cared enough to guide us, to pick us up when we are down, to kick us in the butt when we are wrong, and pat us on the back when we've done well—the people who had faith in us when we lacked faith in ourselves.

"If you don't see those faces when you look in the mirror, then you are missing the picture completely. You are not a self-made man. You are the sum total and the byproduct of everyone who has ever shown up in your life in a positive way."

Lisa was on a roll.

"Think about all the people who have stopped by and poured a little bit of themselves into you—leaving you better than they found you. Some were there for a moment and some for a lifetime. So if you want to talk about heroes, you know plenty of them. That would be a good place to start with in your little speech."

I let her words sink in. She was telling me that heroes appear all the time in the real world, but we often fail to recognize their heroic roles in our lives because they don't wear flashy costumes, throw fireballs, or leap tall buildings in a single bound.

Instead, they alter the course of our lives, not with superhero powers but with superhuman powers.

No one moves up in life without human encouragement. A helping hand here. A kick in the pants there.

Lisa's words resonated in my mind: "Think about all the people who have stopped by and poured a little bit of themselves into you—leaving you better than they found you."

So that's what a true hero looks like, I thought.

A hero looks like the boss who patiently guided a struggling street kid into adulthood.

A hero looks like the spouse who sees the good in you when you can't see it in yourself.

A hero looks like the entrepreneurial family who took a chance on a raw recruit and gave him all he needed to prosper and flourish.

A hero looks like the parent who loves you unconditionally while waiting for you to love yourself.

It wasn't the first time Lisa opened my eyes to something I'd been blind to, and it certainly wouldn't be the last. I wrote my speech with this new understanding of what it meant to be a real-life hero. I wanted to build on what Lisa had told me. I kept asking myself, "What does a hero look like?"

I closed my eyes, visualizing the people who had helped me along the way. I rose from my desk and went to a mirror. (I always keep a mirror nearby, you know, just in case I need someone like me to talk to.)

KEVIN D. BROWN

I stared at myself for an uncomfortable amount of time. I noticed so many new gray hairs, not to mention hairs in places I've never had hairs. But I digress.

Minutes ticked by and the image of my face began to fade. Crystallizing before me were the faces of my heroes. I saw my father. I saw my favorite teachers, preachers, friends, and family. I saw coworkers and colleagues and even the faces of a few people I barely knew who had in some small way made a difference in my day.

With these portraits foremost in my mind, I pondered the question that was begging for an answer: What does a hero look like?

I was stuck. How do you define such a group of people? All of them are different. Each of them had a special quality of some kind. Every one of them had made a unique contribution.

What was the common thread? I began to raise this question to friends, neighbors, people in airports. Everywhere I went, I asked random people what a hero looks like to them.

I wanted to know the qualities and characteristics of a hero. Why do we place certain individuals on a pedestal? Who refuses to be put in the "ordinary" box?

In my boyhood neighborhood, the kids lived for the day when someone bought a washer, dryer, or refrigerator and then put the huge boxes on the curb. To the adults, those boxes were just ordinary containers to be tossed aside. To us, those boxes had unlimited potential!

My friends and I turned those boxes into space rockets, the Alamo, or phone booths where we could change into our Superman costumes! If the girls wanted to play, we turned them into castles, fancy coaches, or phone booths where they could change into their Wonder Woman costumes!

We were limited only by the boundaries of our imagination. And our imaginations ran wild. We spent hours decorating those ordinary boxes, transforming them and delighting in them. They became time machines, in the literal sense, because we would lose all track of time and place while playing in them.

Sad to say that many kids grow into adults who lose their abilities to use their imaginations in that way. They can no longer see beyond the moment, dream beyond the ordinary, or hope for the extraordinary.

And as a result, they get trapped in a box for the rest of their lives. They exist in a very confined and unadorned space. Don't allow that to happen to you. If you feel trapped in a box, use your imagination to break out. Don't conform to the box, transform the box.

Splash your color, your uniqueness, and your best thinking all over that box. Paint with broad brushstrokes of creativity, diversity, and perspective. All the adornments that stop us in our tracks so we can admire the work. We dole out hard-earned money to businesses and organizations whose people have never lost the ability to decorate the box they live and work in. In their hearts, they know what it means to refuse the ordinary and embrace their unique gifts.

7

THE EVERYDAY
HEROES AMONG US

IT'S TIME NOW TO SHIFT gears and put a framework around this idea of being a hero. While working on my hero speech, I came up with a list of the Four Characteristics of Real-Life Heroes. These are four traits that I think every hero has, but over the years I've added many more special qualities that I've observed in most, if not all true-life heroes. We call it "The HERO Effect®," and it is all about being your best when it matters the most. These four qualities will empower you to unleash the best version of yourself and rise higher at work and in life.

For more than a decade, I have been around the globe looking for those who exhibit these four qualities in their work and life—everyday heroes who show up and make life better. After all, that's what heroes do. They make life better.

Let's take a look at each of these characteristics and how they show up in everyday life.

Four Characteristics of Everyday Heroes

1. Real-life heroes always do whatever they can to help others . . . with no strings attached, meaning the only reward they seek is to fully deploy their gifts in service to others. They take the extra steps and go the extra mile, which is only one more step than everyone else is willing to take.

2. Real-life heroes create an exceptional experience for those they serve and serve with. They focus on *transformational* relationships rather than *transactional* moments. They transcend conditions and focus on connections.

3. Real-life heroes are the first to raise their hands and take responsibility for creating the best outcomes. They are accountable for their attitudes, actions, and results. They refuse to be ordinary in any way or at any time. They even do ordinary things in extraordinary ways.

4. Real-life heroes see life and each other through the lens of optimism and abundance.

Think about our guy Richard and how his response reflected all four of those characteristics.

1. His service to Mrs. Johnston went beyond ordinary because repairing that family artifact on his own time was not part of his job.

2. Richard used his gifts to serve Mrs. Johnston and alleviate some of her grief because he sensed what that piano bench meant to her. He created an exceptional experience.

3. Mrs. Johnston and her son were so grateful to Richard because he took responsibility and went beyond what their transaction (or contract) established and did something that transformed their short-term business relationship into a lasting and profound personal relationship.

4. When Richard went into Mrs. Johnston's devastated home, he didn't talk about what a mess it was and how difficult it would be to clean it up. Instead, he assured her that he and his team could make it even better than it had been. Where others might have seen a ravaged house and a scarcity of hope, he saw an opportunity to make a difference and leave Mrs. Johnston feeling much better about her home and her life.

The more I thought about those four foundational characteristics of real-life heroes, the more I became aware of them when we crossed paths. I became much more sensitive to those who bring those qualities to the table day in and day out. My hero radar, call it "hero-dar" if you must, has become highly tuned.

It's like when you buy a car and suddenly you notice there are a lot of the same model in the same color everywhere you go. Or if you buy a loud Hawaiian shirt thinking it's unique and then you go to a party or restaurant and it seems like every other guy has on the same darned shirt.

While looking for heroes to talk about in my speech, I just became hyperaware of people who go out of their way to be extraordinary, whether it's a friend who cheers you up or lends a hand; a business contact who is always helpful and encouraging; or even a clerk in a store who provides an unusually high level of service.

As a franchise sales and marketing guy for many years, I've always been impressed with the outstanding service at Chick-fil-A restaurants, although I go crazy trying to get the name of the place spelled right whenever I write it. If they'd stuck with the original name, Dwarf Grill, my spelling challenges would not be so bad, but I think my appetite for their food might not be the same.

Now I know a lot of folks don't agree with their politics or moral stances on certain issues. And quite frankly that's fine. I am not here to endorse or discuss their politics. I am here to share my thoughts on a business model and a brand that quietly became a giant in their industry.

Let's instead focus on the goodness that is on display in the young men and women who work in their stores. I am one of the many rabid customers who "Eat Mor Chikin" because we always know their chicken will be tasty and their service will be top-notch.

Whenever I pull up to the drive-up speaker at my local Chick-fil-A, I hear a friendly voice cheerfully say, "Welcome to Chick-fil-A. My name is . . . It will be my *pleasure* to serve you." Then there is always a warm greeting from the person handing your food to you. They always say, "Thank you," so I thank them back and then I get: "Of course, sir. It was my pleasure!"

Are you kidding? That's two "my pleasures" in one drive-thru! I know they train them to say that, but I always feel they do appreciate my business. If I am having a bad day, I will go to the Chick-fil-A and order one item at a time. That way I can get six or eight "my pleasures" in one trip.

I also admire the fact that Chick-fil-A restaurants don't open on Sundays so their employees can be with their families. Even their restaurants in sports stadiums stay closed on Sundays.

The "closed Sunday" concept is admirable, but, honestly, there have been many Sundays when I wish they were open. When I get a hankering for one of their sandwiches, there are no substitutes.

So I've thought about starting my own franchise operation called Chik-fil-Sund-A's. My plan is to put one across the street from every

Chick-fil-A restaurant to catch their overflow business Monday through Saturday and then totally dominate that market every Sunday. Watch out Chick-fil-A!

A Cut Above

The Chick-fil-A founder is a hero to many in business because of the extraordinary service his restaurants offer. This remarkable franchise operation understands the power of "and then some," which is the extra-mile mindset. They give their customer an exceptional experience—and then some.

Their brand gave us not only a terrific chicken sandwich but also teens and other employees with good manners. I am particularly impressed with their teenage workers and their excellent attitudes, which I believe are the brand's greatest contribution to humankind.

Listen, the Chick-fil-A team members include kids from the same labor pool that everyone else in their space hires from. These kids are hanging out at the same malls and going to the same schools, but something happens when they join the team at Chick-fil-A.

Chick-fil-A knows that the secret sauce is their culture. The driving force behind great brands comes from within. They instill their service mentality in every employee, and the results have been extraordinary. The environment is one that models the behavior on the inside of the organization that it desires to flow outside the organization.

A healthy and thriving culture is the hallmark of great companies, great communities, and great families. I was blessed to spend nearly two decades with a great brand, a family-owned business that no one really knew about—until they did. That company went from virtual obscurity to the number one brand in their industry in a short period of time.

With more than eighteen hundred franchises when I retired and annual revenues exceeding two billion dollars, that little family business became an industry giant. And we're not talking about some luxury or lifestyle brand either.

This is a hard-core service business that literally digs success out of the rubble. They help people put their lives back together following a disaster—hardworking men and women who go to work every day to help people and make a positive difference.

This is what I think a billion dollar brand–building blueprint looks like.

1. Be clear about who you are.

2. Be brilliant at what you do.

3. Be easy to do business with.

4. Be exceptional every time you show up.

5. Keep it simple.

6. Learn how to tell your story well.

7. Attract the right people.

8. Put them in the right roles.

9. Reward them well.

10. Love everybody.

Obviously, there are strategic, tactical, and philosophical components to building an extraordinary brand. But these ten things should drive every strategy, tactic, and mindset throughout the organization.

Why?

Because they provide a foundation for a culture that is rich in creativity, energy, and focus. A business brand is nothing more than an outward expression of an inner condition. In an organization, that inner condition is the culture.

A culture reflects the experience inside and outside the organization; how we treat one another is how we treat the world.

For an individual, the inner condition is attitude. Whatever is going on inside is what will show up on the outside. Bad service, bad attitudes, and bad luck are all hallmarks of a poor inner condition.

Most organizations love to write their mission, vision, and purpose on the walls. They are proud to line the hallways and staircases with gold letters and impressive-sounding words fashioned together to form pure poetry in the minds of their authors.

The truth is, for many organizations, those words are written to serve as marketing copy to impress the outside world and convince others of their nobility and awesomeness. The great ones, companies we admire and do business with, provide extraordinary service.

A strong service-oriented culture drives every action and every result. Chick-fil-A hires from the same labor pool as every other fast-food restaurant in your town and mine. They aren't growing these people on some island and importing them to hometowns near you. No. They are bringing them into an environment in which they can be the best versions of themselves.

The best business and organizational leaders create an environment in which people can be the best version of themselves. They treat their employees the same way they want their employees to treat their customers.

Your competition can do what you do. They can make the same widgets and offer the same service. They have access to resources, capital, people, and everything they need to compete in your space. And if your business is like most, there are a lot more competitors vying for business these days.

If you really want to differentiate yourself in the market, then focus on culture. Decide now what your obsession will be. Cull the DNA that makes your company great and hone it.

Polish it until it becomes a shining example of what a healthy culture looks like. This is how the great ones attract more qualified candidates than they can employ and have raving fans lining up to do business with them.

The best businesses and organizations understand that other people can do what you do. But they can never be who you are. The businesses and the people who stand out are always a cut above.

Heroes are often portrayed as being bold, brave, and fearless. Maybe some of the flashier "super" heroes are. Most of those I've come across have shared a different trait, empathy. They are sensitive to the feelings and needs of others. They care about how you feel when they meet you. They relate to you.

I know that doesn't sound as heroic as running into a burning building to save someone, or swooping in on a Spidey web to break up a mugging, but I'm here to tell you that these everyday heroes are every bit as wonderful and remarkable as those who are celebrated in movies and city hall ceremonies.

While working on my speech, I found everyday heroes in all sorts of places: gas stations, grocery stores, drive-thru restaurants, and dry-cleaning shops. You may find this next one a little strange, but, well, when I went to get my hair cut a while back, I discovered a terrific example of someone who possessed all four of the characteristics I'd identified.

This is a person who rises above and goes beyond the ordinary into the extraordinary. (And no, I didn't find her at *Super*cuts.) From the moment I first met her, I could tell that she rises above the ordinary in everything she does. She definitely is dedicated to serving others. She takes responsibility for her attitude, actions, and the results they generate. And she has an optimistic spirit, which proved to be absolutely vital when she took one look at the disaster that is my hair.

First a little history: every day of my life has been a bad-hair day. Since childhood, hair-care professionals have treated me like a wad of gum in a wig factory. Seems my hair is hard to cut. Some have likened it to tightly wrapped coils of barbed wire.

As a result, I've paid for more bad haircuts than Billy Ray and Miley put together. Before I met Rebekah, I was really considering shaving my head with a steel hacksaw and selling my shorn scraps to the makers of Brillo pads.

Lisa finally tired of my moaning and groaning and went on a search for someone with the skills of Edward Scissorhands to be my "stylist."

"I found someone to cut your hair," she said before handing me a business card. "This woman served a five-year apprenticeship shearing yaks in Tibet, so I think she can handle you."

Her name was Rebekah, which didn't sound Tibetan, but you never know. I made an appointment and showed up feeling more like I was going in for a colonoscopy than a haircut.

The waiting area was packed, which seemed like a good sign. I didn't see any bloody ears on the floor, which is something I always look for when I go to a new shop.

I walked up to the reception area and caught the eye of one of the stylists who gave me a smile so warm I thought maybe her boyfriend was standing behind me. She had big blue eyes and beautiful dark hair, and I hoped she wasn't Rebekah because I didn't want this lovely lady to ever hate me or my hair.

She extended a hand. "Hi, I'm Rebekah," she said, without a trace of a Tibetan accent. (Good one Lisa, you got me!)

"Hi, I'm . . ."

"*Kevin!*"

"How did you know?"

"Oh, your wife described your hair *perfectly!*"

Despite that, she took me by the hand and led me back to her chair. I've seen a lot of movies involving people strapped to chairs being tortured. Rebekah's chair didn't look quite as dangerous as those in the horror flicks, but I did a quick check for buzz saws under the counter as she draped a fancy cape over me and tied it around my neck.

She moved like a ninja and lulled me into compliance with light banter and a shoulder and neck massage that turned me into a man puddle.

"So, tell me about yourself, Keeeeevin," she teased. "How long you been married? Any kiddos? You look like a banker, are you a banker? I could use a banker on my friend list."

She had me laughing and smiling so much I nearly forgot what I was doing there or who I was. Should I check my driver's license?

Other hairstylists always seemed to be checking their phones or talking to someone other than me while butchering my hair. Rebekah was fully focused on the job, snipping with an artistic flair while keeping me entertained.

She did not text, tweet, or post a single selfie while I was her captive. I liked being her captive. She laughed at my jokes.

No one laughs at my jokes.

I was actually disappointed when she put her scissors down, stepped back, and looked at me as if I was a work of art she'd completed. Then, she gracefully pulled off my fancy cape without letting a hair hit the floor, flashed a smile, pointed at the big mirror on the wall, and said, "What do you think, *Mr. Delicious*?"

I blushed. (That *never* happens.)

"Do you call all of your male customers Mr. Delicious?"

"Oh no, you are my one and only Mr. Delicious."

"Wow, I'm honored. How about the shoulder rubs? Do you give all of your customers shoulder rubs?"

Rebekah smiled coyly.

"Yes, sir. Everyone in my chair gets that right away to help them relax from the stress of the day," she said, before slyly adding, "Lisa said you'd like that part because you are kind of uptight."

"Well, it certainly worked for me, Rebekah, and you are now my hair hero!"

Mr. Delicious took his haircut home with a smile on his face. By the way, I've since tried several times to get my wife to call me Mr. Delicious. You can probably guess how that's gone for me.

Now, you may want to call me out for hailing Rebekah a hero just because she is an excellent hair stylist who also happens to be very good at flattering a certain extra-needy middle-aged guy.

And you may have a point there.

Except, I might argue that everyday heroes do not have to have special powers or flashy costumes. In my view, they are women and men and children who strive to be better and do better while making life better for those around them.

Rebekah made my life better. She removed my stress and distracted me from the pressures of the day. My types of heroes are from all walks of life. If they are in business, they rise above the competition. They build mutually beneficial and lasting relationships with their customers, as well as with their employees, their suppliers, and maybe even their competitors.

They may not call their customers and clients Mr. or Mrs. Delicious. In fact, under most circumstances, that would just be weird. And, just to be clear, the name is already taken. By me.

I would drive by at least twenty hair salons to get to Rebekah's, and most of the others are less expensive. But when your hair stylist is a hero, saving a couple of dollars doesn't matter. Rebekah's exceptional service is worth the drive and the extra dollars. She refuses to be anything but exceptional.

The great ones always want to be *the* choice not simply *a* choice. She drew me in with a simple smile. And then made me feel like I was the only person in the room.

Do you make the people you say are the most important to you feel like they are the only people in the room? Your only priority? Or are they simply one more thing to check off your list for the day?

The Nonnegotiables

Rebekah's operating philosophy starts with a nonnegotiable mindset. The playbook for how she decided to run her life and her business begins with a foundation of how she *chooses* to treat people. For her, it's nonnegotiable.

I find this to be a common thread with heroes. They treat everyone well, and they know that every moment matters. I came to Rebekah to complete a transaction—a good haircut for a good price. But she *transcended* our agreement by making the experience so enjoyable and by establishing a personal connection.

Unfortunately, most people are focused on the nonessentials. They tend to get caught up in low payoff activities. They are busier than everyone else, just ask them. And when the day is done they have accomplished very little while still facing a mountain of to-dos.

Many people and organizations operate from a transactional perspective, meaning they are focused on the conditions of the contract: "I will do this for you, if you do this for me." Their covenant is to perform the minimum required to get by. They focus on things that are not really important, such as making excuses or the busywork and fake priorities they come up with that keep them from creating an above-and-beyond experience for those they serve.

The nonessentials are *anything* that doesn't move your priorities forward. It's anything that distracts and detracts you from bringing your best stuff to the present moment and pouring it into the lives of others.

Heroes think differently. They aren't focused on contracts and conditions. Instead, they intentionally focus on making real connections with the people they serve. Heroes reach beyond what is required to achieve what is remarkable.

Think about people who've touched your life in positive ways. Do they have the four characteristics I've identified? What else do your heroes have in common? What other characteristics do they share?

What about you? What can you do to be extraordinary in every aspect of your life, especially in your interactions with others?

What can you do to serve others with no expectation of a reward?

What will it take to elevate your transactional moments into transformational relationships?

And, finally, how can you bring the healing and energizing light of optimism into your life and the lives of others?

The truth is, our operating system for daily living is created by design or by default, and it's 100 percent our choice to decide which system to deploy. When we operate by default, we let the winds of change and the opinions of others guide us. As a result, we are aimlessly tossed from one moment to the next. We have no purpose and no control. When we operate by choice, we take control and follow our purpose. We take complete responsibility for our results, no matter what happens. We choose how we want to show up every day, or whether we want to show up at all. We have the final say on how we deploy our gifts and how we make an impact.

I want to challenge you. Right here. Right now.

Are you willing use the talents and abilities you were endowed with at birth to give those around you an experience they cannot get from anyone else?

Are you willing to dig deep and uncover the superpowers within you and use them as a force for good in the world?

Are you ready to break free from ordinary thinking and grab hold of the exceptional life you were designed for? Well then, let's get to work!

8

JOSH-BROWN
AND
"AUNT BEA"

YOU MAY FIND IT SURPRISING that one of the highlights of the speech I eventually prepared for our annual convention was about a hero my family discovered at Disney World.

No, it was not Prince Charming, or Snow White, or any of the make-believe characters. This was a real-life everyday hero, someone who came into my family's life and exhibited all four of the hero characteristics I've identified—and many more.

What makes this story particularly compelling and inspiring is that this hero's actions transformed not only our lives but also her own—in ways that none of us might have imagined.

To set up this story, I want to tell you first about our son, because there is something about him that I have not shared with you yet in this book. His name is Josh, as I mentioned earlier, but if you met him, he would tell you that his name is Josh-Brown.

One word. Hyphenated. But always one word in his mind.

Josh-Brown has his own way of seeing the world. As his parents, we have learned a great deal from his perspective on life. When our son was just three years old, Lisa and I became concerned that his speech and language skills weren't developing as they should. We gave him time to grow at his own pace but also kept checking in with our doctors.

Then, when Josh-Brown was five years old, we gathered in a school conference room with teachers on one side of a big mahogany table and doctors on the other. We were scared young parents, and we knew these people were about to confirm what we had long suspected but were afraid to say out loud.

Josh-Brown was on the autism spectrum.

"Mr. and Mrs. Brown, we are sorry to inform you that your son has autism. You need to understand what that means for him and for the two of you looking ahead. This will be a long, hard journey for you and your son. He won't learn like the other kids. He will be uneducable in some ways. It is not likely that he will graduate high school. If he does, it will most likely be with a special education diploma."

Big tears dropped on the papers resting in Lisa's lap.

I stopped listening, struggling to control my anger.

I began thinking about all the things our son might not do. I am embarrassed to admit it, but at that moment, I was mostly sorry for myself, and angry because the life I had hoped to live vicariously through my boy had just vanished. He would not be a star Little League shortstop like I was, or quarterback of the high school football team, like I was not.

My dreams were smashed. While I was having a pity party for one, Lisa was already out of the blocks and moving forward on a less selfish and more positive track.

Her tears dried up. Her jaw set. I knew that determined look. She had kicked into Mama Bear mode. Nobody was telling her what her cub could do or not do. I watched as a leader with the title of mother leaped into action. She did what real leaders do; she took the storyline that life had just given us and went to work rewriting it. She looked at her son and said, "Cover your ears, Josh. Don't you listen to him. What he said about you is not your destiny. Mom has a different plan for you."

Lisa heard the diagnosis but rejected the prognosis.

I am amazed at how many people go through life accepting the storyline they are given instead of writing their own. They get up every day and follow it as though an inauthentic story is their truth. They are content to accept labels put on them by others, or they accept someone else's opinion as the final word. Remember, the pen is always in your hand. You should feel free to write your own story, one that allows you to fulfill your God-given potential.

Lisa had a greater vision for our son than the limited vision of the other people in that room. She wasn't about to accept their labels or their limitations. Her fierce advocacy proved to be a life-changer for our son and our family. We all have the power and, dare I say, the responsibility to reject the ordinary path in life.

My wife did not simply nod and go along with the prognosis that our son's life would be determined by the label of "autistic." She rejected the ordinary path and chose to take us on an extraordinary journey.

We all have the power to make that choice. You have it. I have it. I recommend that you never accept the limitations imposed on you by someone else—and certainly do not impose them on yourself. I did that in my teens and early twenties, and then I had a lot of catching up to do when others convinced me of my greater potential.

In the case of our son, Lisa did not waste a moment grieving over our lost dreams. She focused instead on helping Josh discover his dreams by equipping him to exceed any and all expectations. This is the essence of leadership.

The label "autism" meant nothing to her. She saw to it that our son's life would not be restricted or defined by anyone else. I'll never forget the first time we heard Josh refer to himself as "disabled." We rushed to set him straight.

Honestly, I don't think my feet touched the floor as I went to him—and Lisa beat me there.

"Where did you hear that?" she asked him.

"At school."

Lisa squatted to be at his eye level, held his face in her hands, and said, "You are not disabled, Josh-Brown. You may have some challenges, but you don't have disabilities. In fact, you have special abilities because you are a special boy, so don't ever use that word to describe yourself."

I know far too many people who allow their poor attitudes to disable them from pursuing their best lives.

The Heroic Parent

Lisa became our son's indefatigable advocate. She created and enacted a strategy to explore all possibilities and opportunities, tracking down the best teachers, tutors, mentors, and coaches for him. She found a holistic doctor in Tampa who specializes in treating those with autism. He became an important member of Team Josh-Brown, and he continues to work with our son to this day.

Lisa scoured every available resource to learn about therapies, treatments, and programs that could help Josh. She stepped up as a leader and accepted the responsibility for his care and development.

She made some very helpful discoveries along the way. She learned that diet and nutrition can be important factors for those with autism, affecting how they learn, develop, and perform.

She put Josh on the GFCF diet (gluten and casein free) when he was six years old. She turned our kitchen into a commercial grade bakery that would make even super chef Emeril Lagasse green with envy. *Bam!*

She cooked and baked everything for her boy. From bread and snacks to cakes and treats, she was all in.

Lisa also cooked treats for the teachers and staff at his school. She began taking care of the people who would take care of our son. It was her way of thanking them in advance for their work with Josh and a strong signal that we would be active participants in this process.

No sideline parenting here. We worked side by side with the educators to help draw out the best version of our son. After all, that's what it means to educate: to draw out.

This included drawing out our shy son socially. When Josh was in middle school, Lisa made sure he became active in the school's chapter of Best Buddies, the international nonprofit organization founded by Anthony Shriver that supports those with intellectual and developmental challenges by building a community of volunteers and creating social and employment opportunities.

Basically, their program pairs up typical kids with special needs kids to encourage one-on-one friendships. They go on outings like pizza parties, bowling matches, kickball games, and ice-cream socials.

Josh gained so much confidence he decided to go out for the junior high's football team. He was taller than a lot of kids but still very scrawny at that point. So he settled for being team manager.

But even in that role, he was injured during a practice. Our son was holding a blocking dummy when one of the players decided to tackle it, breaking Josh's arm. We weren't happy, but it seemed to make Josh feel even more like a part of the team.

We worried that he would become more isolated in high school because there was no Best Buddies program there. Can you guess who stepped in and started one? Yes, Lisa a.k.a. Mama Bear founded a chapter there.

Thanks to her efforts, Josh attended a prom put on by Best Buddies in Nashville. There were three thousand kids there. Josh took the stage to do one of his favorite things. He gave a weather forecast that was played on the arena's JumboTron screen. He felt famous and very happy. As he often noted, it was a big deal.

Best Buddies introduced him to a lot of kids whom he would remain friends with through high school. Some of our favorite memories are seeing our son attend birthday parties with twenty or thirty other kids from his school and neighborhood.

Lisa worked closely with all of our son's teachers and school administrators so that he could be a mainstream student. She accomplished this working with an individual education plan (IEP). These custom-designed plans help teachers use the most appropriate materials and approaches, including modified lesson plans and tests, for special-needs students like our son.

Lisa pretty much lived at his school, volunteering, baking cookies, running concessions while also working with his teachers to make sure they followed his IEP and that it was working for him.

Josh is at the higher end of the autism spectrum but still quite different and quirky compared to most of his classmates. He is also shy, so we worried that he might become isolated in high school, which tends to be a tougher environment for kids like our son.

Lisa and I even decided at one point that after middle school we would place him to a private school for his high school years so he could get more specialized attention. We spent weeks looking at private schools and finally found one that we both thought would be great.

Our plan had one major flaw. We hadn't asked our son what he wanted. This is a lesson I learned in business but failed to apply at home. Leaders can tend to put people where they need them, instead of talking to them about where they might flourish and make the strongest contribution.

The ideal would be to place people in positions where they could make the most of their talents and knowledge so they could continue to grow while contributing at the highest levels. Imagine what joy everyone could bring to their work if they had that opportunity.

Our son was not shy about telling us how he felt about going to a private school rather than the public high school where his classmates were headed.

"I want to stay in my school with all of my friends," he said.

There was no changing his mind, and, as it turned out, Josh-Brown had the right plan. We had worried that as teenagers enter the last years of school, they get physically stronger and the hormones kick in, which means that bullying becomes more of a real threat.

Josh had experienced some locker room bullying in middle school, but we dealt with it quickly. I kept a close eye on him after that, checking in with him daily, while also looking at his social media to make sure no one was preying on him.

You learn a lot about people when you see them through the eyes of my son. Actually, let me expand on that. You learn a lot about *the world* when you see it through the eyes of our son.

Josh is never cynical or jaded. He sees the best in people and believes there is good in everyone. He may appear to be naive, but I see him more as full of hope and optimism. He focuses on what is possible instead of what is probable.

Our son also believes that anything is within reach, which is a credit to his mother's loving and caring guidance. No matter what goals he sets for himself, Josh is always convinced he can achieve them.

When he sets his sights on something, you don't want to stand in his way. Especially if his sights are set on Disney World.

Josh-Brown's Dream Vacation

When Josh was seven, he discovered the wonderful world of Disney, and he quickly became enthralled with everything in the house of the mouse. Kids with autism tend to obsess on certain things. Josh focused on going to Disney World. He was relentless.

Lisa, who has Disney Princess levels of optimism and positivity—little birds do land on her shoulders—decreed that our son was just "passionately encouraging us."

We held off going until September of 2007 when Josh-Brown was nine because we wanted him to be old enough to enjoy and remember all the Magic Kingdom had to offer.

I was sure this trip would satisfy his Disney desires for at least a year or two.

What a Goofy thought that was!

My plans to get some work done on this trip were also way off the mark. I was on the workaholic workout back then. I've never been a good vacation taker. For most of my (allegedly) adult life I have suffered from chronic overstriving. I thought family vacations were for everybody in our family but me.

Even at home, I couldn't help myself. Lisa often thought she was married to a laptop. I would come home from work and spend "family time" sitting with them but staring at a computer screen.

Present but not accounted for. Lisa had to wean me from my computer. It was a painful process: my fingers kept reaching for the keyboard, so she had to get a ruler and smack them.

My name is Kevin, and I'm a recovered laptopaholic. I finally broke free, and I encourage you to do the same. Your job will end one day. You will want your family to still be there, won't you?

When you are with them, *be* with them. A friend of mine always says, "Be where you're at!" That is good advice and very, very bad grammar. I'm not a grammar nazi, but I will stick with "Be present."

I hadn't learned that lesson back when we first took Josh-Brown to Disney World. I brought my laptop thinking he and Lisa could hit the park while I ran the office remotely.

I'd not considered that Lisa plans vacations with the same precision as NASA's exploration of Mars. She is a numbers cruncher. She's never met a spreadsheet she couldn't dominate.

Josh likes routines and schedules too. They are the perfect traveling tag team.

Lisa had every minute filled with activities, making sure Josh-Brown could hit all four parks: Epcot, Hollywood Studios, Animal Kingdom, and the Magic Kingdom. We were set to conquer Everest, Kilimanjaro, and Space Mountain. She was determined that Josh-Brown ride every teapot, train, and roller coaster.

I was about to learn that Disney is not a small world, after all!

We had to pack an extra suitcase with Lisa's spreadsheets before heading off to the airport for our flight to Orlando. We arrived late in the afternoon.

I was thinking a nap might be in order.

"Dad, there will be no napping!"

Or sleeping. We had to do a scouting trip to identify the fastest route to the park and all of its enticements. We may have set a land speed record as our son dragged us through all four parks, identifying key landmarks and potential points of contact with Mickey and friends.

The kid was wound up. He reminded me of an old Disney commercial featuring a little boy lying in bed the night before entering the park of his dreams. His eyes were closed, but he was awake and giggling to himself.

His mom whispered, "Honey, you have to go to sleep."

The little boy kept his eyes tightly closed and said, "But I'm so excited!"

Josh-Brown was that little boy, and I have to admit, his enthusiasm was contagious. None of us slept the first night, but I only giggled once.

Do you remember what it was like to be so excited that you couldn't sleep? Unfortunately we grow up and trade our excitement and enthusiasm for stress and worry. As adults, we still can't sleep, but it's mostly because of dread and fretting instead of excitement and enthusiasm. Still, it's within our power to change that, isn't it?

Our children remind us of what it was like to be young and joyful. My son has a few challenges, but he never lacks the capacity for joy and excitement. That is just one of his gifts.

The Magic (Kingdom) Chef

Disney may cause pain in the pocketbook, but their long history of providing the highest levels of hospitality and entertainment has always intrigued me as a leader and as someone who often speaks to corporations and organizations.

I had to admire Disney's brand mastery from a marketing standpoint. The folks who run that show have made it a magical experience for their guests. As a parent, I'm particularly impressed by how they can make my life savings magically disappear.

But let's not think too much about that.

I am a really ugly crier.

I entered Disney World with my wife and son for family fun but also to observe firsthand how they put the brand magic into their theme parks, restaurants, and hotels. I made this a work/play trip of sorts.

I did learn a great deal about how Disney manages to take so much of your money and leave you smiling, at least until the credit card bill arrives. What I had not anticipated was meeting a Disney World employee who would become a hero to my son and our entire family.

Thanks to this caring and empathetic person, our very own Josh-Brown became something of a big deal in the Disney culture, believe it or not! An unofficial brand ambassador for Mr. Mouse.

So, let me tell you about a Disney experience that even today makes me smile and reflect on all that is good not only inside ol' Walt's world but within society itself. Having a son like ours provides many lessons and insights into both the bad and the good of human nature.

This story embodies all four of the hero characteristics and serves as a shining example of what it means to be your best when it matters the most.

Josh-Brown has superpowers when it comes to bringing out the kindness in people—and the good Lord knows his father can always use help with that.

On our first full day at Disney World, the Brown family was up and at 'em bright and early.

"Dad! Dad! C'mon, get up. We have a big day ahead!"

"Where do you want to have breakfast?" I asked the man with the plan.

"Dad! Don't you remember the schedule? Today, we are eating downstairs in this hotel, of course," he said. "That way you don't have to complain about walking too far, riding a train, or standing in line. We are easing you into the program!"

Josh-Brown knows his father well.

We arrived at the restaurant where a cheerful hostess greeted us with a warm smile and said, "Welcome, Brown family! We are so glad you are here. We have a table just for you."

Personal touches and sunny demeanor matter, I thought, making my first business note of the day. (I hope the IRS auditor is paying attention here.)

Our new hostess best friend took us to our own special table and distributed menus before flittering away with another charming line: "Brown family, may I be the first to wish you a magical day!"

Wow, a magical day! That's brilliant. These folks are really good!

Reader, please note: it gets better. This was not even the Disney person who became so important to our family, but she was a great warm-up. There was, however, a brief interlude of not-so-magical service.

Enter our server. Let's just give her the benefit of the doubt and think maybe she was having a bad day. Maybe her car wouldn't start that morning, or she missed the bus, or maybe she'd had to deal with a surly guest just before arriving at our table.

Maybe she hadn't gotten the memo that she was working in "the happiest place on earth."

I have learned that heroes who perform at high levels rise above their challenges and deliver their best no matter what is going on inside. Disney is one of the best in the world at delivering pleasurable customer experiences, so I expected anyone working for this legendary brand to be gracious and accommodating.

Whatever was going on with Miss(ing) Personality, she was a rare disappointment in the service department. No warm greeting. No charming repartee. Not a smile but a scowl. Let's just say, she put the curt in courtesy.

"Can I get you something to drink?"

Now, whenever we go out to eat with Josh-Brown, this is where Lisa steps in and explains that our son has special dietary needs. Lisa had learned early on that those with autism have delicate digestive systems. Josh-Brown was gluten and dairy free long before so many others climbed on that train.

"Yes, we would like some drinks, but I want to let you know that our son is on a special diet and there are a lot of things he can't have . . . ," Lisa began.

Our server stopped Lisa's explanation by raising a hand in the air as if she was on safety patrol and halting traffic.

The silent command was: "Halt. Stop talking."

"If that's the case, I cannot take your order. You will need to speak to the executive chef," she said.

Then she marched off without another word.

Somebody missed her fairy-dusting appointment, I thought.

The bar was set high for this trip, admittedly. Given the cost and the global brand on the entry sign, I expected more than courtesy and five-star service. I wanted people who whistled while they worked! I expected small birds landing on our shoulders everywhere we went.

Our server was a great reminder that even in one of the greatest corporate cultures on the planet, all "cast members" make a personal choice on how to show up for the people they serve and serve with.

Lisa knew I was irritated. She leaned over and said, "Honey, let me handle this. I don't need Captain Freak-Out ruining the first day of Josh's magical adventure."

I bit my tongue, but I was steaming from the ears and eyeballs as I watched our sullen server depart. I scanned the vast dining room, looking for a supervisor to heckle when my laser vision honed in on a Chef Boyardee hat bouncing our way.

This must be the aforementioned executive chef, my laser brain noted.

While the server trailed a cloud of gloom, the chef seemed to have a saintly glow of radiance lighting her path to our table. Upon arrival, she flashed a 200-watt smile, looked at my son and said, "Good morning, Sunshine!"

Josh-Brown is very shy by nature. His response to this lovely greeting was controlled by his shyness. He lowered his head and muttered, "Good morning."

Undaunted, the chef continued cheerily: "My name is Bea. I understand we have someone on a special diet. How can I help?"

Lisa informed her that our son was on a gluten-free diet, which was not as common back then as it is these days. In fact, Chef Bea had never worked with the gluten-free flour that can be used to make meals for those with food allergies like Josh-Brown.

While Lisa explained how she made gluten-free meals at home, Chef Bea whipped out a notebook and a pen and scribbled notes. When Lisa had finished her list, the chef studied her notes intently and then fired off a series of questions.

Great team members are brilliant at asking questions. She was enthusiastically listening, probing in search of ways to provide better service delivered in amazing ways.

I could tell that Chef Bea was a step above, a dedicated Disney team member who was hot on the case, eager to serve a guest's needs.

"What other gluten-free ingredients do you use at home? Where do you get that brand? How do you make that?"

Josh-Brown perked up when Chef Bea looked at him and asked sweetly: "What is your favorite breakfast, Sunshine?"

There was no delay in his response.

"Apple pancakes, please!"

Chef Bea's smile warped just slightly at our son's enthusiastic order.

"Oh, Sunshine, I am so sorry. I don't have the ingredients to make your apple pancakes special like your mom does," she said. "I don't have the correct ingredients right now. How about some bacon and eggs with some special toast just for you?"

Josh-Brown seemed okay with that.

His wise father knows this because he said, "Okay."

Chef Bea flashed another warm ray our way, nodded farewell and light-beamed her way back to the kitchen.

Miss(ing) Personality returned to take the rest of our order. She later delivered it with all of the enthusiasm of a roadside vending machine.

The breakfast was excellent, however, and once we were nourished, the Browns scampered off to the Magic Kingdom, where Josh-Brown gleefully explored his Nirvana until his father and mother were ready to drop.

Mothers often say that there is no tired like pregnancy tired. I think Disney tired might be a close second. When night descended, and we hit the pillows, we slept like we'd fallen under a spell.

Day Two Was a Bea-uty

"Dad! Dad! Let's go! We have so much more to see today!"

"Okay, Josh. But first, where are we having breakfast today?"

"New plan, Dad! I want to go back and see Aunt Bea!"

My groggy brain flashed to a black-and-white image of a matronly country lady sporting a beehive hairdo in the Mayberry days of *The Andy Griffith Show.*

"Aunt Bea?"

I looked at Lisa in confusion.

It's a look she knows all too well.

"From yesterday's breakfast, dunderhead," she said, using a term of endearment. "Remember, that nice executive chef? Her name was Bea."

"Oh, right," I said as the fog cleared.

Then I asked Josh-Brown, "Buddy, what about your plan? Are we really going off-plan this early in the game?"

Josh-Brown was not to be messed with. He was on a mission.

"Dad! I want to go see Aunt Bea!"

Apparently, any breakfast by Bea was acceptable in Josh-Brown's world.

There was one problem. Our planner in chief, Lisa, had made a reservation for breakfast at another location that morning. But our son had his heart set on seeing his favorite chef, so we headed downstairs to try our luck.

"Good morning Brown family? I see you don't have a reservation, but that isn't a problem! In fact, I have a table just for you," said the sunny hostess.

I'm sure you do, I thought.

After our special dietary demands the previous day, I feared we would be seated in the "problem guest" area with Scrooge McDuck and maybe a retired Cruella De Vil or two.

Instead, she took us to the same table where we'd been seated the first day. I had a flashback of surliness, so I looked up and spied our sullen server from day one. She spied me too and made a (forgive me, please) Bea line into the kitchen.

I was still focused on the kitchen door when out popped Aunt Bea/ Chef Bea. Within seconds, she was beaming her Bea-ness onto the Brown family.

"Good morning Sunshine!" she said to our son.

"Good morning," said Josh-Brown shyly.

"What's for breakfast, Sunshine?"

"Apple pancakes, please!" said Josh hopefully.

"You got it, my dear. No problem!"

I was stunned. I assumed that she had forgotten about Josh-Brown's special diet.

"Time out, Aunt Bea. Do you remember us from yesterday?"

"Yes, sir. I do."

"But yesterday you didn't have the ingredients to make apple pancakes."

"I'll explain in a second, but first, why are you calling me Aunt Bea?"

"That's a fair question. Sorry, can't answer it right now. . . . Yesterday you didn't have the ingredients."

"True."

"Today you do?"

"Yes."

"Where did you get them?"

"The store."

"Oh. So you sent someone to the store?"

"No, sir. I stopped on my way home and shopped for all of the gluten-free brands your wife told me about. You do know that we have grocery stores *all over* Florida, don't you? Anyone can go."

She was teasing me, but I was amazed by what I had just heard. The executive chef of a Disney restaurant had gone shopping for ingredients just for Josh-Brown? I mean, Lisa and I shop for him all the time, but I wouldn't ask anyone else to do it, let alone a big-time Disney chef.

This was taking customer service beyond all expectations. As a guest who is also a marketing guy, I was floored.

So I asked Chef Bea, "Why would you do that?"

"Well, Josh-Brown said he wanted apple pancakes!"

Just then, a server arrived with a huge plate of apple pancakes shaped like Mickey Mouse ears. Our son was ecstatic. We were blown away.

Instantly, I made a "note to self" that said: Give the customer what they want or need, whether we serve it or not. Travel the extra mile.

Chef Bea demonstrated that there is always a way to deliver an exceptional experience for those you serve. No excuses. No blame. She was committed to doing all she could do to deliver excellence.

This was a level of customer service above and beyond all expectations. Right then and there, Josh-Brown and his parents became fans for life of both Chef Bea and Disney World.

Josh-Brown only stopped smiling long enough to gobble down his apple pancakes. (There were no leftovers, sorry.)

If you asked any of our family where else you can get a good breakfast at Disney World, we could not tell you. We ate with Chef Bea for the next seven mornings.

If Josh-Brown could have figured out how to kidnap his "Aunt Bea" and take her home with us, I might have gone along with it. We were that impressed with her, and our appreciation of this woman wasn't just about her delicious food.

Chef Bea became a hero in our eyes because:

1. She refused to be ordinary in her approach to her job.

2. She provided extraordinary service with no expectation of a reward.

3. She rose above the typical transactional meal for money deal to create a transformational relationship that continues to this day.

4. And she radiated a contagious optimism and abundance whenever we met with her.

When we returned home from our vacation at Disney World, we bought a thank-you card for Chef Bea. Josh-Brown signed it as did Lisa and I. We also sent her a "tip" for her trip to the grocery store for apple pancake ingredients. And I wrote a letter raving about our experience with her to all of Chef Bea's Disney bosses.

Always keep in mind; there are only two times in life that people talk about you. When you exceed their expectations or when you miss them completely. And I bet you can guess when they like to talk about you the most.

The minute you drop the ball or miss the mark, your customers or clients will tweet that little gem out to the world. Focus on giving those you serve something remarkable to talk about. Enthusiastic ambassadors for your brand will tell your story better than you ever could.

We talked about Chef Bea for weeks, and every time we discussed what she had done, we were all the more appreciative and amazed. In fact, Josh-Brown wanted to send her an even bigger tip, so we sent another thank-you card with more cash.

Yes, Disney was still costing me a fortune, but the truth is, we were happy to pay a premium for such accommodating service. Mostly, though, we valued the heroic character of this kind and empathetic woman whom Josh-Brown still calls "Aunt Bea."

She could have gone home that first day and put her feet up, knowing she'd served us a great breakfast. We had no complaints. Instead, Chef Bea made the choice to go to the grocery store and buy the special ingredients for our son's apple pancakes.

Now keep in mind, Chef Bea had no idea if we'd even return for breakfast that week. Our plan had been to try several different restaurants during our stay. But this woman and our nine-year-old son had made a connection. Josh-Brown certainly felt that way because he demanded we return to her dining hall.

There is much more to our story with this amazing women. I will share the rest with you in a bit. Rest assured that Chef Bea has become a permanent part of our family. Josh-Brown connects with her at every opportunity—and he has a lot of opportunities to do that these days.

It's also interesting that while our first-day server left a poor impression, we forgot all about that once Chef Bea showed up. So one shining light can help overcome all of the dimmer bulbs in a business—something that is worth keeping in mind.

Being extraordinary is your responsibility and your choice every day.

Heroes choose wisely. For with great power comes the enormous responsibility to develop yourself and use your gifts to change the people around you in some positive way.

Heroes make life better for everyone within their reach. That's the entire job description. They make life better at work and at home. They show up intentionally every day. Nothing is random. There is no such thing as coincidence or blind luck.

They set out to make a difference. They want to bring sunshine and encouragement to everyone on the team.

I get really frustrated when I hear people talk about random acts of kindness. We celebrate the goodness in people and we should. But we should not celebrate that it was random. Bringing light to darkness, joy to those in despair, and hope to the hopeless should never be left to the whim of our mood. We should, instead, be focused on creating positive outcomes.

Using our gifts and superpowers to move people from where they are to someplace new. Someplace better.

What if you had a daily agenda centered on the positive impact you wanted to have on everyone you encounter? Wouldn't that be better than getting wrapped up in the pettiness so often found in the workplace or social media or even the dinner table? What if you focused on making better connections with those around you instead of making your relationships conditional?

9

A LASTING
IMPRESSION

IN MAY OF 2016, ABOUT nine years after our first family trip to Disney World, Lisa and I were invited to a high school graduation ceremony near our Tennessee home.

Hundreds of people packed an arena to watch nearly three hundred high school seniors receive their diplomas. We were seated with friends and family in the upper deck.

The aspiring graduates marched into the arena, striding to their seats in unison. They walked in a single file, wearing their caps and gowns. Lisa and I watched intently for one particular person. He was easy for us to spot. Standing nearly six feet tall with his cap a little crooked was our amazing and heroic son.

After Josh-Brown reached his seat, he turned and looked for us in the upper deck. He spotted us, gave a quick nod, and took his seat with his graduating classmates.

Then the principal called out their names one by one. When the name Joshua Douglas Brown was announced, our son rose from his chair.

Tears welled up in our eyes. The hairs on the back of my neck stood up. We were so excited for our boy who had come so far.

Josh had walked a hero's journey, without any doubt. My wife had served as his biggest advocate and champion. I was so proud and happy for the both of them. Lisa's vision and Josh's destiny were being fulfilled in that moment.

Watching Josh graduate from high school was one of the most powerful moments I have ever experienced. I couldn't take my eyes off him. I wanted this moment etched in my memory forever.

I could tell that Josh-Brown was savoring the ceremony too. He stood in the line of classmates with his back straight, head held high, and looking forward. He fussed a little to make sure his cap and gown were straight. When they handed him his hard-earned diploma, he proudly grabbed the honors cords draped around his neck.

Oh, our shy son walked with a swagger that day, and he seemed to grow taller with every step. Our cheers and applause were joined by many others who'd played roles in Josh-Brown's education and accomplishments. You weren't supposed to make any noise, but we all broke that rule for this special occasion.

Lisa and I were sobbing. We could hardly see as we walked down to join him and take photographs. All of my photos were blurred because I was shaking so much.

He hugged his mom first, as he should have. She was the encourager who told him that he had special abilities. She created the greater vision and helped him fulfill it.

That moment reminded me of my father's advice when I was a boy. Whenever I struggled with the opinions of others or when someone told me I couldn't do something, my dad would always say, "It doesn't matter what anyone else *thinks*. All that matters is what you *believe*."

To repeat: it does not matter what anyone else thinks of your potential. All that matters is what you believe. Believing in something is powerful. And when you believe, I mean really believe, you activate unseen forces to help you manifest the reality you seek.

Lisa instilled that spirit of self-determination in our son. I can't tell you how many experts told us he would not graduate from a mainstream high school. They didn't think he'd ever be admitted to a college either. But they were wrong on both counts.

They failed to consider what Josh believed about himself. Those experts weren't with him and Lisa for the countless late-night study sessions. They weren't present when our son put his head in his hands and asked, "Why doesn't my brain work?"

And, they weren't there when his mother leaned down and whispered in his ear, "Honey, your brain is just fine. Being special just takes a little more work!"

You see, leadership isn't easy. Mentoring someone to greatness isn't easy. Winning in life isn't easy. If it were easy everyone would do it. The truth is, it's hard.

You have to get down in the trenches and do the work of a leader. You have to get better before you can ever help someone else find the best version of themselves. And there will be times in the process when the people you are trying to help won't like you.

Thankfully leadership isn't about popularity. It's about potential. Ironically, when you help someone find their true potential you become a popular leader.

Back to Our Future

When we returned home after graduation, Josh, Lisa, and I sat at the dinner table. We took turns looking at his diploma as if it were a magical thing. And it was.

Josh-Brown smiled and said, "I did good, right?"

"Man, you did better than good," I said. "Your mom and I are very proud of you. To reward you for this great achievement, we want to take you on a trip. Anywhere you want to go in the world. Personally, I'm hoping for Australia, but the destination is *yours* to choose."

Without hesitation, our high school graduate Class of 2016 looked at me and said, "Dad, I want to go see Aunt Bea."

I squinted at him, tilted my head slightly, and said, "You're kidding me."

"Nope. I really want to go see Aunt Bea."

"Okay, we will work on making that happen, my boy."

Two months later, the Brown family returned to Aunt Bea World, known by some as Walt Disney World in Orlando. Lisa the planning queen had arranged for us to spend the morning in the park and then to connect with Josh-Brown's favorite chef at the Hollywood Studios restaurant, Hollywood & Vine.

By then, Bea had been a Disney cast member for more than twenty years. We were not surprised that she had moved up in the ranks, but we did not know, at that point, the role our son played in her story.

When we arrived at the restaurant, we had to wade through a huge crowd outside. It turned out that Handy Manny, a character from a popular Disney Channel show, was appearing at the restaurant that morning.

"What name is your reservation under?" asked the restaurant host.

"We don't have a reservation," I said.

"Sir, I'm sorry. We are jam-packed because it's a meet-and-greet day for Handy Manny, and his fans have us booked solid for lunch. I don't have a table for you."

"But we have a lunch date with Aunt—I mean Chef—Bea!"

This seemed to confuse the host.

"I'm sorry," he said.

I turned to my wife and son. Josh was tapping frantically on my arm. This typically means that he has something important to tell me.

"Dad, Dad, what just happened?"

"Well, we don't have a reservation, and they don't have any extra tables because of Handy Manny's fans."

This did not placate Josh-Brown.

"You need to do something, Dad."

So I leaped into action just as I always do in critical times.

I looked at Lisa.

Lisa looked at me.

"You need to do something, *Dad*," she said.

Did I detect a note of scorn in her tone?

She was calling me out.

I returned to the host stand, boldly going forth to meet the challenge.

"Please, please, please, please can you find us a table?" I begged. "We are supposed to meet with Chef Bea!"

Yes, I played the Bea card.

Shamelessly.

He seemed unmoved. So I went dark.

"I will give you everything in my wallet. Name your price. I have to get in there!"

"Sir, I can't make any promises. But let me check."

I wasn't sure if it was the proposed tip or sheer pity that moved him. And I didn't care.

He returned a few minutes later and handed me what appeared to be a hockey puck with lights on it.

No, it was a restaurant pager. I figured that out all by myself.

"I can get you in, but it will be at least forty-five minutes," he said.

My heart soared.

Then, he added: "We still won't have a table for you, and you won't get to eat, but you can say hello to Chef Bea somewhere in a corner or hallway."

"We will take it!"

"Okay, what's your name so I can write it down?"

"Tell Bea that it's Josh-Brown, and he is here for apple pancakes!"

A light went on in his brain. I saw it. Really, I did.

For the first time, he flashed a smile at me.

We found a seat in the waiting area among the Handy Manny hordes. In less than two minutes, I looked up to find a sharp-looking guy hovering over me. He wore a Secret Service sort of earpiece. I thought maybe he was a Disney security dude. Or, possibly, CIA. He looked very professional.

He leaned down and whispered in my ear like he was asking for a secret password.

"Are you the apple-pancakes family?"

Playing along, I said, "Actually, we call ourselves the Apple-Pancakes Gang."

The man from Disney then extended his hand toward my son.

"You must be Josh-Brown. My name is Mike. You are famous around here. Please follow me."

Josh-Brown looked at me curiously.

I knew what he was thinking.

What? Me? Famous?

There was no time to discuss. The man from Disney was slicing through the throngs, urging us to follow.

We gathered our things and hurried behind our new friend. The Handy Manny fans looked at us, wondering if we were celebrities, or perhaps Disney insiders.

We weren't used to special treatment, so we felt a little awkward. That passed. Then we began to feel special. Well, I did anyway.

I put on my VIP strut. I may have waved at a few onlookers. Mr. Big Shot coming through!

The man from Disney led us into the restaurant and then to a corner of the lobby where he stopped and stepped aside to reveal . . .

Aunt Bea!

In the flesh!

For the record, I did not break out in song, but the lyrics from "Oh Happy Day" did play out in my brain.

Josh-Brown, who normally doesn't show much emotion or initiate physical contact, walked up to his hero and fell into her arms.

They hugged for what seemed like an hour.

Lisa was in tears. I was in tears. We were crying, taking pictures, and completely absorbed in the joy of this moment.

And then my pesky business brain kicked in with a question.

How does Chef Bea do that? How can she connect with someone on a level that transcends business, special needs, and a decade in time?

I studied this saintly woman with kind eyes and a magical smile. I wondered: How did she create a moment nine years ago that made our son want to celebrate his graduation with a woman he'd only met briefly when he was still in grade school? How was it that Chef Bea had transformed a business relationship into a personal friendship?

Those questions and many more were answered when we sat down for more than an hour and talked with Chef Bea. We learned that there was much more to the apple-pancakes story than we'd ever dreamed.

The Ripple Effect of Kindness Unleashed

This is what she told us that day: "Mr. and Mrs. Brown, you probably don't know that when you were here in 2007, I didn't know anything at all about autism," she said. "I am passionate about what I do, and I love serving people. From that day until now, I have not stopped learning about the effects of food on children with autism. I cannot thank you enough for what your son has done to make me better."

Let that sink in. This humble woman who'd had such a positive impact on our son, Lisa, and me was telling us that Josh-Brown had helped make *her* better?

You see, something always lingers when our lives intersect with others. The question is, what lingers when you leave? What do you leave behind after a meeting or a phone call? Your reputation can be a powerful force in your life, for better or for worse; it precedes your physical presence and remains in your place after you are gone.

I normally travel two hundred or more days a year speaking and consulting with clients. I see people moving through airports completely unaware of their brand message. In fact, I'm convinced that most people do not have mirrors in their homes. They roll off the assembly line and give little thought to their packaging and messaging for the day. What does your personal branding say about you? Do you draw people in and leave them wanting more or are you barely noticed at all?

More and more, I was realizing that Chef Bea is a great chef and an exceptional human being.

She then took my admiration to an even higher level on that day.

"Another thing you probably don't know is that when we met in 2007, Disney wasn't really equipped to handle special dietary meals for kids like Josh-Brown," she added. "After your visit, we went to work and created a program to serve kids like him, and I am happy to report that in 2016, we will serve over one million kids with special dietary needs like Josh. We can't thank you enough for what your son has done for our business."

Our entire family entered the shock-and-awe stage. The ripple effect from our first meeting with Chef Bea had touched the lives of over one million other kids!

She then explained why we'd been made to feel so special by the Disney cast when they realized we were the Apple-Pancakes Family.

"I have shared the apple-pancakes story at employee meetings and with all my teammates," Chef Bea said. "We aspire for the apple-pancakes experience to be the gold standard for how we serve our customers in all of our restaurants."

We had often told friends and family about our first encounter with Chef Bea. I had incorporated the story into my motivational speeches and shared it with thousands of people over those nine years. It was one of the stories that people seemed to remember the most and take into their hearts.

And now, we had learned that that same story had become part of the Disney corporate culture through our Aunt Bea connection! Wow!

We spent a lot of time talking with Chef Bea and learning that influence is always a two-way street. Each of us has the potential to be of benefit and to benefit from every interaction.

There is great power in that. Chef Bea seemed to know this instinctively. It is what elevated our experience with her from the transactional to the transformative level. She is an extraordinary person, a real-life hero to my family and thousands of others.

When you are focused on making life better for the people you serve and serve with, I believe you unleash the forces of creativity and imagination. You will find new and better ways to create an exceptional experience. You will find those tiny touch points where you can do small things with big intentions that distinguish you from your competition. You create magical moments that have the power to change everything.

The Bea Attitudes

Chef Bea is a hero because she refused to be ordinary. She listened with empathy and then went above and beyond to serve others. Her actions transformed a part of the Disney culture. She optimistically believed in her ability to make a positive change for her guests and her employer.

By listening to the needs expressed by my son and my wife, Chef Bea made one of the world's most highly regarded brands even better. You may never know the positive influence that you can have on others.

Josh-Brown didn't, until his hero Chef Bea told him.

Since that visit with her, I tell all of my audiences that regardless of where you've been or where you are in your life, you have the power to rise above through service to others. Don't wait to be served. Get out there and share your talents and gifts and experience for the benefit of someone else, because if you have a positive impact on them, you can be sure it will benefit you too.

Don't let your gifts go to waste. Never settle for anything less than giving your best and being your best. Fulfill the destiny you were created to achieve. To do that, strength of character is essential. Are your values rooted in bedrock principles like honesty, integrity, fairness, empathy, and respect for others?

If your character is built on those values, then the attitudes you present to others will reflect them. People will sense that you are self-assured, open-minded, and optimistic.

Let's look at the attitudes our real-life Disney hero, Chef Bea, conveyed in our conversations and interactions with her.

BEA AUTHENTIC: The first thing we noticed about Bea was her warm smile, which reflected her character rooted in openness, empathy and humanity. Our server, in contrast, had scowled at us like we were dirty dishes she had to clean up.

I'm sure Chef Bea had a lot of things cooking at work and in her personal life that day, but she took the time to listen carefully and do her best to make us feel like welcome guests rather than problem children. If she was having a bad day, we never would have known it.

Many people drag their personal garbage around everywhere they go. They let their challenges impact their attitudes and spread the misery to everyone around them. Whatever you focus on affects your attitude and your relationships.

Your feelings are real. You don't have to fake being happy if you aren't. Be authentic, but understand that while you can't control how you feel, you can influence how others feel about you.

If you have been kind to them, they will be kind to you when you need their support. If all you've done is unload your garbage on their doorsteps, don't expect them to welcome you inside.

The one proven path to a more positive attitude is to change the focus from your problems to the needs of others. You may feel down, but you can choose to focus on uplifting others, which will also lift up your spirits. Try it!

BEA KIND: Bea radiated kindness from the moment she approached our table. She did not learn it from an HR pamphlet or manual. Her kindness was not manufactured. It came from the heart and was reflected in how she listened to our son to understand his needs.

When he asked for apple pancakes, she could tell by his expression they were his favorite. She paid attention and saw an opportunity to serve an unmet need, not only for our son but also for so many others like him with special dietary needs.

As often happens, her kindness and empathy resulted in wisdom. She made a decision before she ever left our table to respond in an extraordinary way, and as a result, she made a remarkable difference in the lives of many people.

BEA PRESENT: To have a positive impact on others, you have to be present for them, attentive to their feelings as much as their words and focused on understanding rather than being understood.

That is a challenge for many of us today because of so many distractions vying for our attention, including social media, emails, texts, and the devices that deliver them to us 24/7.

Heroes are not dominated by their devices, vices, or every crisis in their lives. Our smart phones, tablets, and other devices pull us away from the present moment. Our vices preoccupy us, and we rush through the present moment. And we can't take every negative event in our lives and blow it up into a personal crisis.

Heroes are present and accounted for. They block out distractions and focus on the task at hand. They live fully in the moment. They understand that nothing is casual and that everything deserves their full attention and focus—not a glancing blow or half-hearted effort.

BEA GRATEFUL: Gratitude is a powerful force. Bea seemed genuinely grateful that we chose to spend our mornings with her. She was thankful for our business and for the opportunity to serve our family. A spirit of gratitude will help clear your mind of garbage thinking that clutters life with problems and pessimism.

BEA EXTRAORDINARY: Some people are simply not willing to be exceptional. They may show up, but they don't stand out. They take their gifts for granted. The heroes in our lives attain that status by developing them, sharing them, and using them for a greater good, as Chef Bea did.

She has the will to go above and beyond, to act upon opportunities, and to rise above challenges. She is willing to find a way when others would say, "No way."

To create an exceptional experience for the people in your life, you must be willing to show up, and show out. This means you have to be there for others and then be willing to share your gifts. Whether on the job or in your personal relationships, you must seek to deliver exceptional results without exception, and without expectations of rewards.

BEA ENTREPRENEURIAL: Chef Bea works for a company founded by one of the greatest entrepreneurs in history. So it is no surprise that she and her fellow Disney cast members have been encouraged to think like entrepreneurs.

Entrepreneurs are all about looking for opportunities to serve the needs of others, whether in business, in their communities, or in their relationships. Yes, you can be an entrepreneur in all three of those areas and more.

After talking to Lisa and Josh-Brown about his special dietary needs, Chef Bea saw an opportunity to serve our son while also expanding Disney's menu to serve an unmet need among all young people with food allergies or diet restrictions. That was a classic entrepreneurial move.

She proved that you can be an entrepreneur even if you work for someone else, by recognizing an area to improve and grow the business. Chef Bea also saw an opportunity to use her experience with our family as a learning experience for her own personal growth. She didn't just listen to us, she went out and learned everything she could about the dietary needs of children like Josh.

Walt Disney himself once said: "The greatest moments in life are not concerned with selfish achievements but rather with the things we do for the people we love and esteem, and whose respect we need."

With his words and Chef Bea's actions in mind, I encourage you to be entrepreneurial in your work and in your life. Look for opportunities to use and grow your gifts to serve the unmet needs of everyone you encounter at work, at home, and in the world around you.

You can be a life entrepreneur like Bea if you embrace:

- Extraordinary levels of self-motivation
- A driving desire to make the most of your gifts and your impact on the world
- Delivering the unexpected *wow* experience for the people you serve
- A commitment to the best possible outcome in every situation
- Owning your results
- The ability to see opportunities where others may only see challenges
- A willingness to take calculated risks by letting go of what is safe and known so that you can grow and find greater fulfillment

- A contagious enthusiasm and passion that attracts others to support and encourage you

I know that each of these life-entrepreneur qualities is important because just seven months after our second meeting with Chef Bea, I put them to the test by making a big bold leap, or two.

10

A BIG BOLD LEAP

CALL ME CRAZY.

You wouldn't be the first.

In December of 2016, I resigned from the greatest job of my life, one that was personally fulfilling and financially rewarding. My bosses had grown what began as a mom-and-pop business into one of the country's biggest franchise operations. They gave a raw kid a chance, mentored me, allowed me to make mistakes, and then promoted me to lead three divisions as only the second non-family member to join the executive team.

I was having a ball. The company was still growing rapidly. There were around seven hundred franchises when I joined, and we were closing in on eighteen hundred. Annual system-wide sales were blowing past the $2 billion mark. I'd come into this company still as a street kid, and they'd helped me become something very close to a polished executive and leader.

I mean, before I knew it, I had more than one suit and one tie in my closet. For a guy who once lived in his car, that's a big deal.

But here's what happened: my boss, Rick, had basically created a speechifying monster by pushing me to speak at company events. After the big convention, I became an in-house celebrity of sorts, the face of the brand within the company.

I believe that is a position every organization should have, by the way. Organizations spend millions of dollars to have celebrities tell their story to the world at large. But what about the customers inside the organization? Who is telling and selling the brand story to the people on the inside of the company? I think it is critical to spread the word throughout the organization, because your team members ultimately serve as your ambassadors to the customers.

I am not exaggerating when I tell you that that speech marked a turning point in my life. I began to receive hundreds of cards and letters from our franchise teams, telling me how much it had uplifted them to see themselves as having the power to be heroes.

Our franchisees were in a dirty and difficult business. Their employees were dealing with disasters daily. They were dispatched to one huge mess after another. The homeowners were often grieving and in deep despair. You could easily get burned out in that sort of environment every day—unless you saw yourself as a force for positive change in the lives of these hurting people; unless you went out every day knowing that you would make a huge difference in their lives. You were helping them to rebuild and restore what had been torn apart. You brought hope to those who felt hopeless.

Here's the really crazy thing: simply by planting that far more empowering image in the minds of our franchise teams with my speech, I became an internal celebrity, of sorts, in our company. It was bizarre. Suddenly, I had rock-star status.

UNLEASHING YOUR HERO

I did not handle it well. It scared me. I felt unworthy.

Whenever I was in large groups where franchisees and employees were, I'd pretend to be on my cell phone so I didn't have to be gracious to people saying nice things to me. (Note to self: make sure you turn off the ringer when you are fake-talking on your cell phone.)

I was a jerk, okay?

Accepting gratitude was something new for me. My old demons still dogged me at times, telling me I was unworthy and a pretender, so I wasn't good at it.

But, deep down inside. I liked it. I *really* liked it.

The owners of the company liked it too. They told me I'd helped elevate the culture of the company and that it was having a positive impact on the system. They promoted me to executive management and gave me an opportunity to create real financial security for my family.

I know, money doesn't buy happiness. I believe that is true. But it sure gives you a running start toward it! It's a big load off your mind to have enough in the bank to cover the bills, treat your family to a vacation, and even tuck away some for the future.

My speech meant to inspire and motivate others turned out to inspire and motivate me in ways I'd never dreamed possible. I began to see the world through an entirely different lens. For the first time, I had a greater vision for my life. I felt I was on the right path.

As my vision crystalized, I flashed back to a lesson David had taught me. He always talked about vision and goals.

"If you can easily accomplish your goals, they are too small," he'd say. "Your vision should be so big that the person you are today cannot get there. In other words, your vison should require you to grow in order to achieve it."

Another unexpected result of that speech: I began to receive invitations, requests, and offers of substantial money to speak to other groups. Eventually, I realized that many of the spouses of our employees and franchise team members had been in the audience for my speech. They'd gone home to their own companies and organizations and recommended me to them.

But I had a day job. I still didn't think of myself as a polished inspirational or motivational speaker. I mean, you wouldn't believe how many people tell me I look like the Wolverine in the X-Men movies. Believe me, they aren't saying I look like the actor Hugh Jackman who plays him. They mean that I look like the big, bad Wolverine.

To me, the only thing that face inspires is fear!

I told the first few people who requested that I speak to their groups: "I appreciate your offer, but I'm really not a professional speaker."

Lisa was not impressed.

"You can't see it, can you?" she said. "You're scared to come out from behind the curtain, even though you love being on the stage. You can't have it both ways!"

Lisa was right, but please don't tell her. Maybe the real me was finally coming out of hiding. But I truly enjoyed crafting a speech and delivering it to an audience. And they seemed to enjoy it too, especially when I talked about them having the capacity to become everyday heroes.

The more I spoke within our company and its franchises, the more offers I received to speak at other companies that had heard about me through the grapevine.

At first, I didn't know how to respond to these requests. I didn't want to take on outside work that might detract from my day job performance. I had a demanding position as it was. I wasn't looking for outside speaking opportunities.

I turned down most of them because I didn't have the time or the energy, but the offers kept coming. More people showed up as encouragers, one after the other. As I mentioned earlier, my former boss David was one of those people. Lisa, certainly, and the Isaacsons, founders of SERVPRO, too.

Next up, was organizational development expert John G. Miller, the author of *QBQ! The Question Behind the Question.* John is the leading authority on personal accountability, as well as a great friend and mentor to me. We both spoke at our convention in 2005, and a couple weeks later, he called me.

"I don't know if this means anything, but I watched your speech and I think you could do this professionally," he said.

Now, John is a very smart and successful guy and for him to call and encourage me was like someone turning on a light in the darkness, pointing out a path and saying, "You need to go there."

By that point, I'd learned to pay attention to the encouragers who come into my life. Often, they prove to be heroes. I recommend that you do the same, especially if you are just embarking on a career or a second career or chasing a dream.

I believe that when you find something you were truly meant to do, these supportive people show up in your life. It's funny how we often tend to take criticism to heart but shrug off compliments or encouragement. Everyone wants to be recognized and validated.

I saw an interview with Oprah Winfrey in which she talked about this.

"What common thread do you find running through the lives of all the successful people you've interviewed?" she was asked.

Oprah replied that whether it was Beyoncé whether it was Beyoncé or presidents Bush or Obama, "when the cameras stopped rolling and the lights were turned off, they all leaned over and said, 'Was that okay?'"

Each of them wanted to know if they had done well. They wanted to be validated. They wanted a little encouragement from the woman herself that they'd done a good job in their Oprah moments. Don't you want to shine in the moments that matter the most to you? What could be better than knowing you've nailed it with your best work when everything is on the line?

The answer by the way is always yes. Those around you are counting on you to deliver excellence every time you show up. Heroes always bring their "A" game, not simply "a" game.

Oprah also attached three questions that I think are brilliant. She said that she believes everyone is silently asking these three questions.

1. Do you see me?

2. Do you hear me?

3. Does what I say even mean anything to you at all?

Wow. Think about those questions and ask yourself: Who in my life is asking those three questions? Better yet, how am I answering them?

I believe there is a competition for your time and attention in every relationship, whether it's customers and colleagues or your significant other and your children. If you can't answer those three questions they are asking with a resounding yes, well then you have left the door open for someone else to serve those relationships better than you are serving them.

Everyone seeks validation and encouragement. There's no shame in seeking it, but there is far more power in giving it. I'm not asking you to perform "random acts of kindness." I think kindness should be intentional and habitual. Not random. You should treat people kindly because empathy and caring is part of your DNA.

Now, I get that it is easy to be kind when everything is going your way. You may not be inclined to be kind when the wolves are at your door. But remember, kindness is a superpower. It is also a choice.

Making other people feel good will make you feel even better. As someone who spent a decade struggling to find a path out of despair, I have a special appreciation for those who were kind to me and encouraged me. They helped me believe in myself, and in humanity. That transformation is nothing short of a miracle, because there were many dark days in my teen years when I considered just ending it all.

Lighting the Way

I was grateful for John Miller's guidance, and I certainly did not expect him to follow up with an opportunity to work together a few weeks later. He was getting so many speaking requests that he couldn't possibly do them all, so he offered to partner up with me. I began doing even more outside speaking events thanks to his referrals.

These engagements gave me the opportunity to try out new material and refine my speaking skills. I was learning a new trade. I still had my day job, which I loved, but once I found that I could make audiences laugh, well, I was hooked. Me funny? The lost boy? The struggling street kid?

Hearing the laughter and applause of an audience was almost a spiritual experience. I felt someone was tapping me on the shoulder and saying, "I have another plan for you."

Mere humans were tapping too. In 2014, a friend recommended me as a speaker to Troy Peple, founder of a business development firm that was holding an event in Nashville. After I spoke, Troy came up and asked to have his photo taken with me.

"I don't normally do this, but I think you will be somebody one day," he said.

He then recommended that I connect with a well-known speaker's bureau based in Illinois. He made the introduction, and a week later, I was invited to participate in one of their events.

"We are doing a showcase for our speakers in early 2015," their representative said. "We have one spot left. It's five hundred dollars plus expenses."

I told him that I hadn't done of lot of paid speaking engagements.

"No, *you* pay us."

Turns out, this was more like a tryout. They wanted to see if I had the goods before recommending me to their clients as a speaker. And so I found myself in Springfield, Illinois, standing in front of two hundred people—all representatives of companies that hire speakers from this bureau.

"You have twenty minutes to show your best stuff," they told me.

I quickly became aware that I was the only nonprofessional of all the speakers in the lineup. I recognized a lot of them as speakers I'd hired or tried to hire for events.

When I looked in a mirror before stepping on stage, I saw all of those who'd served as my champions and supporters. Their numbers seemed to be growing by the minute. My fear of public speaking melted away. Instead, I felt humble and grateful for all of these heroes in my life.

You are welcome to try this at home. It's something I learned that day and I've used it ever since. The next time you are confronted with a challenge, think of it as an opportunity instead. Don't let any challenge become your kryptonite. Turn it into your power drink instead by seeing it as an opportunity to rise above and go beyond.

Heroes are often referred to as larger than life. Everyday heroes are larger than life's problems. They find the strength and courage to confront their fears, doubts, and insecurities.

When a young man put the microphone on me that day, he said, "Break a leg!"

I've never understood why people say that—or, worse, "Knock 'em dead!"

I gave the guy a wink and said, "Not today. No broken legs here. We are going to knock 'em alive!"

My superpowered self-talk kicked in. I was filled with excitement, and I could feel it moving through me in a way that energized me and made me feel unstoppable.

When you care about the people you serve, you want to show up and give them an experience they won't soon forget. The next time you feel like you've taken on too much work, say to yourself, "But how lucky I am to be given so much opportunity that others would love to have."

It's about what you get to do instead of what you have to do.

This can work as an instant attitude adjustment. It has certainly helped me fight off the demons of fear and self-doubt over the years since. This simple mindset shift turns anxiety into an advantage. I've realized that I don't have to conquer the world. I just have to convince myself that the world is really on my side.

Gratitude filled my heart as I walked out on stage to deliver twenty minutes of my best stuff. I went out there pumped up to kick butt. And apparently, I didn't stink.

They signed me to their bureau then and there. Within weeks they'd lined up nearly twenty speaking engagements for me all because of my twenty-minute speech.

I was floored by this debut and so were the folks at the bureau. They called it a "booking bonanza."

And that is when everything changed.

Over the next year, I had about forty more paid speaking engagements. Most of the time, I'd have to fly in and return home the same night because I was still running three divisions for my real job.

By the end of 2016, I had run myself ragged.

My day job was still very fulfilling and rewarding. My bosses and coworkers were like family. But there was nothing like taking the stage and working to inspire, entertain, and enlighten an audience. As someone who'd been slow to realize my own potential, I found purpose in guiding others to achieve their dreams.

Lisa and I had prayed about the next move. She had given up her career to be a full-time advocate for Josh-Brown. So I was the sole provider and looking at a big pay cut. No more healthcare benefits and no job security.

Earlier that year I'd asked God to help me understand which career path to take. I think His position had become clear.

The time had come for my leap of faith.

Now to be clear, I am not a big fan of "follow your heart" or "just do what you love" career-planning advice. You have to make a living. At least most of us do. So before taking a leap, you should practice some smaller jumps, or try leaping with a safety net in place.

Lisa and I had always lived below our means even in the best times. We had a comfortable nest egg in savings. I also felt confident that if a speaking career did not work out, I could return to either my old job or another marketing job. My dad always told me to never burn a bridge because some day I might have to walk back across it.

Even so, this was not an easy decision. The hardest part was sitting down with the owners, who had been so good to me. It was a bittersweet parting for me, but they were supportive, as always.

I didn't have anyone pin a towel "cape" around my neck this time. I had no delusions that I was Superman. Even so, I kept flashing back to my childhood leap off the garage, hoping the landing wouldn't be nearly as painful.

To my surprise, it wasn't.

In my first year as a full-time professional speaker, I had more than a hundred engagements. I went from being a rookie to a major league player in the industry and built a substantial speaking business in a few short years. I am still stunned and extremely grateful for how well it went when I took this leap. I didn't hit the driveway this time! My landing was soft. And no one showed up to spank me!

Meanwhile, my former work family was soaring too. In 2019, three years after I left, they sold majority stake to a private equity firm, for an estimated $1 billion.

I hadn't seen that coming. I was happy for my friends and so proud of the work everyone in the company had done to take the business to the next level. They climbed from humble beginnings to incredible heights.

Their new platform will give rise to a new generation of entrepreneurs and help change the family trees of many of my friends who are still there. In fact, my own family tree would have changed financially forever, had I stayed.

Some have asked if I regret leaving. Nope. I keep telling myself I am right where I am supposed to be. The sound that you are hearing might be a man quietly weeping, but pay no attention.

Just kidding. I have no regrets, because this new career has paid dividends in many ways that have nothing to do with material wealth. My leap of faith has led to even more fulfilling relationships and fun in my family life.

You see, there was still one more major move for the Browns to make.

The Sunshine State

In 2019, I had a speaking engagement in Clearwater Beach, Florida, over Valentine's Day weekend. Lisa came along for some fun in the sun and so we could have our traditional romantic dinner on the holiday for lovers.

I figured out early in my speaking career that my wife always offers to come along if I'm headed to a venue that offer toes-in-sand opportunities. She has never been to Cedar Rapids with me. Or Topeka, Kansas.

While in Clearwater, we went out for a wonderful dinner at Blinkers Beachside Steakhouse and Lounge. We were enjoying a nightcap when the conversation turned to our one and only son, the wondrous Josh-Brown, who would be hitting his twenty-first birthday in a few weeks.

He was out of school by then, living with us and working part-time. Our son had exceeded all expectations and risen above the limitations and labels that came with autism, mostly thanks to his hard work and Lisa's devoted parenting.

Over Valentine's Day dinner, we talked about what was next for him. Lisa became emotional.

"He doesn't seem happy, and it breaks my heart," she said, brushing back tears.

I was concerned for our son too. But in that moment, I also became concerned about my own safety. This was a romantic venue on what is supposedly the holiday to celebrate love and stuff. My wife was crying and everyone in the restaurant was giving me the stink eye, assuming that I was causing her heartbreak and ruining romance for all the other couples.

A vision flashed in my mind. I could jump up and assure everyone that Lisa was crying tears of joy over our happy marriage. Bad idea, I know. I stifled it.

Back to Josh-Brown. I agreed with Lisa. Our adult son needed more positive stimulation and more joy in his life than his doting parents could provide.

"I think he needs a greater sense of purpose," I said to Lisa. "What could we do to give him that? What do you think would excite him about life and give him more joy?"

"Disney," she said.

My first thought was, "This is going to cost me."

My second thought was, "She's right!"

Josh-Brown has two passions. The weather and Disney. He is a self-described "Disney freak and weather geek."

Another thought flashed in my mind. I should have snuffed it, but I blurted it out instead:

"Let's move to Florida!"

"You are crazy!"

She then pointed out that while our son loved Disney, he did not like change of any kind.

"Gallatin is the only place he's ever lived," she noted. "I don't think he'd respond well if we took him away from his comfort zone."

"You may be right," I said. "But he's an adult now, so let's give him a chance to decide."

(In case you are wondering, I did make it out of the restaurant without being punched in the face for spoiling any other guy's Valentine's Day plans.)

After we returned to Gallatin, Lisa and I waited for a good time and then pitched our relocation idea to Josh, knowing that he might hate it.

"How would you feel about moving?" Lisa asked.

He lowered his head and stared at the floor, not saying a word.

Not a good sign.

But then I added the kicker.

"To Orlando?"

Josh launched out of his chair and did a little dance.

"Dad, that's always been my second home! *Disney* is there!"

He then went galloping up the stairs to start packing.

So that settled *that*!

Lessons Learned

Four months later, we moved into the beautiful chain of lakes community of Windermere. Lisa and I had looked at thirty homes in three days. We bought the last one we saw, in part because it had a separate suite where Josh-Brown could feel independent and set up his makeshift weather studio.

Even better for him, our house is just a fifteen-minute drive from the main entrance of the house of the Mouse. Within two weeks, he bought an annual pass to all of Walt's theme parks. Believe me, Josh-Brown gets his money's worth out of that pass.

His dedication to Disney serves as proof that your passions are more powerful than your fears. Our son is not comfortable in crowds unless they are Disney crowds. His love of theme parks is so powerful he is willing to rise above his anxieties and fears and spend entire days with thousands of strangers.

Social distancing comes naturally to him, so when the coronavirus hit and Disney put special safety rules in place, we never worried about Josh following them. He acquired a vast collection of Disney-branded face masks and wore them with delight.

His current routine is to visit Disney World at least twice a week. He has joined a large group of bloggers and podcasters who are passionate about all things Disney. In fact, he has become quite the blogger and a budding podcaster, using skills he's taught himself. He acts as a roving reporter when visiting the parks. He also has a passion for weather and offers up a central Florida forecast every night. It is amazing to watch his true identity emerge.

New parents like to think that they will spend the next twenty years or more teaching their babies the ways of the world. Most of us realize eventually that our children teach us perhaps even more than we can teach them. This has been especially true with our son.

As a person with autism who is relatively high on the spectrum, Josh-Brown is unique in many ways. He sees the world in a far more restricted context than his parents and most other people. We like to think we see "the big picture." Josh's perspective is more like a big screen with many small pictures inside it. Imagine that you are on a Zoom call with ten people instead of one. There are a lot of boxes to deal with, rather than just one, so you have to focus on just one at a time.

Our son tends to focus mostly on all the realms of the Magic Kingdom and on weather systems around the globe. Those are his passions. He blogs, creates videos, and works on podcasts about those topics with a dedication and depth of knowledge that boggles the mind.

Lisa and I are hoping that one day he can build a career around his passions. In fact, if the Disney folks every decide to create a theme park called The Wonderful World of Weather, we have an outstanding candidate for the CEO position.

Josh is in his early twenties now, and I'm still learning about his unique perspectives, his challenges, and his gifts. When we tell him that he has special abilities rather than disabilities, we are speaking the truth.

Our son surprises us every day with his special abilities, whether it's his instant recall of exact dates and times for past events, or his self-taught skills with computers and social media. I've applied many of the lessons I've learned from our efforts to guide him while he guides us.

I identified five leadership lessons I learned from Josh-Brown that I applied when I was an executive, and I often share them when I speak to businesses and organizations.

The Josh-Brown Rules of Leadership

1. **Determine the best way to communicate with each member of your team.** Some people need it in writing. Some need to hear it. Josh has difficulty reading, but if you thoroughly explain things to him verbally he does much better. He also is very literal, so he doesn't get jokes, sarcasm, or buzzwords.

    Be clear. The job of a leader is to communicate with absolute clarity and make sure that understanding takes place. Too often in business we speak in code, hiding behind corporate clichés and innuendo. True leaders share compelling stories that motivate and inspire people to take action and conquer their goals.

2. **Lay out each expectation, project, or goal.** Define the steps. Explain the rewards. Remove any barriers to completion. Josh has always had chores around the house, and he also helps Lisa and me by running errands. We have learned to give him very clear guidance on what we expect him to do and how we expect it to be done. We lay out the steps and procedures and clear the way for him to succeed.

3. **Help your team members focus intently on one big singular objective and explain to them how smaller goals lead to it.** Josh cannot multitask. He isn't programmed that way. But when he is focused on something, he becomes totally fixated on it. We learned to apply that special ability to his school work when we gave him one goal at a time. Does it work in business too? Yes!

4. **Don't just tell your team what to do, show them what getting it right looks like.** Josh has trouble with fine-motor skills such as buttoning shirts. So Lisa actually made cardboard shirt templates with big buttons on them so she could demonstrate to him how to button and unbutton his shirts. Since he is a visual learner, this helped him a great deal. Like Josh, most people tend to do what they see you do rather than what you tell them to do. The great ones, the heroic leaders I know help people to become competent by showing them what success looks like. They model the behavior they seek in those on the team.

5. **Tie goals to their gifts and passions while tapping into each individual's special abilities and gifts.** This will get people engaged and help them find joy in their work. The best move I made was one day asking Josh if he wanted to go jogging with me. He'd always liked to run and he had a lot of energy to burn. I motivated him by challenging him to beat "your old man."

Another incentive we offered was that if he would match my time from my first half-marathon, we would take him back to Disney. He had a goal. The time to match was two hours and ten minutes. He finished that race in *exactly* two hours and ten minutes. On the dot!

I managed to finish before Josh in our first half-marathon together, but he hit the target—and won another trip to Disney in the process. It wasn't long before he was burning right by me every time we competed. I never finished a race before him again. Goals are important. Incentives are imperative. Disney was his "why" to win.

The kid had endurance and speed and the desire to beat any goal I set for him. When his senior year began, I suggested he try running for the cross-country team. This turned out to be the perfect sport for him. In fact, I often wished that he'd gone out for the sport earlier, because though it is a team sport, you compete as an individual.

You don't run against other competitors. You run against the clock. Cross-country was the perfect sport for our son. For the first time, Josh was part of a team, and we all enjoyed cheering him on with the other families and taking our turn providing snacks.

Josh-Brown thrived on the experience. He focused on training so he could better his times. At the end of the cross-country season, Josh earned a letter in his favorite sport. To this day, he stays in great shape by jogging as many as seven miles a day.

I can't keep up with him anymore, and I am perfectly content for him to take the lead.

11

PUTTING ON
THE CAPE

THE HERO'S JOURNEY MY SON traveled was not smooth. Yours probably will not be either. In fact, you will experience plenty of bumps along the way.

Years ago, Josh-Brown, Lisa, and I were on a very bumpy flight from Nashville to Los Angeles. I travel so much, I didn't pay much attention to the turbulence, but my son grew anxious.

Josh was about ten years old and seated between Lisa and me when the plane started to bounce. He reached over and took hold of our hands. Then, he leaned over to me and whispered, "Dad, are there bumpy roads in heaven?"

I loved the innocence of his question, the pure and simple thinking of a young boy when he experienced bumps in the sky.

I leaned over and whispered back, "No, son. There are no bumpy roads in heaven. But the journey can sometimes be rough."

Grown-ups get it. We make plans and outside forces intervene. We get sucker punched, whipsawed, and body-slammed by events and evils beyond our control. A business opportunity falls through. A bank loan is denied. The guy in front of you buys the winning lottery ticket. Your boss gives your job to his nephew who majored in keggers.

You can't control all the crap that comes flying at you. But you can control your next move. And your next and your next and your next. There is power in that! Unbelievable superpower. Heroic power.

To set off your power of self-determination, you need only to fire up the traits of a hero: optimism and abundance. My dad used to say, "Sometimes you're the windshield, and sometimes you're the bug." How true it is. You never know what life will throw in your path. Heroes are always prepared to deal with what comes their way.

I once took our family to see a movie called *A Bug's Life,* a 3D movie. It was a good movie, but without the 3D glasses, it was nothing but a big, blurry screen. We went to the afternoon matinee, and as we sat in our seats, we noticed another couple settling close by with their kids.

There was an argument taking place between the parents. I couldn't help eavesdropping, just a little.

"I'm not putting on those stupid glasses," the father said, sounding more like a cranky teenager than a parent.

"We are here for the children, so put on the glasses," replied his exasperated wife.

Dad the drama queen then threw both hands up in the air like a petulant child and said, "I am not wearing these silly glasses. They will make me look like a dork!"

The Eavesdropper leaned over to Lisa and whispered, "Too late! He should have thought about that before he strapped on his fanny pack."

Lisa shushed me and ordered me to put on my 3D glasses to conceal my identity. She even made me wear them when we were leaving the theater so the guy wouldn't come after me. You know, it hurts when you walk into walls.

Seriously, I think about that childish father when I think about the power of optimism and abundance. The lesson I drew was that without the 3D glasses, the movie looked completely different than it did with the glasses on. So that father did not experience the film in the way its creators intended for us to experience it.

The same is true in life. If we look through the lens of optimism, we see life the way the Creator designed it to be seen: rich, vibrant, and full of color. We see people not as they are but as they can be. Life not as it is but as it should be.

Tragically, without the lens of optimism we begin to see life and people exactly as they are and miss out on their unique contribution to the world. Kids tend to be more optimistic than adults because they haven't experienced disappointments, cruelty, or the worst the world can throw at them.

Adults, on the other hand, tend to be more pessimistic because they have had more negative experiences and interactions. This is like driving forward while looking in the rearview mirror instead of through the car's windshield.

Your rearview mirror only shows you what you've passed. The windshield shows you where you are and what lies ahead.

Whether you are in a car or not, it is dangerous to focus on the past. And not at all productive. This is a lesson that took me a long time to learn because in my younger days, I let the bad things that had happened to me as a teenager make me fearful, pessimistic, and scarcity minded about life.

David was one of those heroes who came into my life and reminded me that fear, pessimism, and scarcity are all negative viewpoints that only hinder our ability to achieve our goals and dreams. He also reminded me that we can choose how we respond to negative emotions.

Imagine if I'd taken those attitudes with me on client calls at a disaster recovery and restoration business: "I'm sorry that your home was flooded, but I'm afraid (fear) that there is nothing we can do to repair it (pessimism), and really, I don't think anyone could ever restore what you had (scarcity)."

We probably would not have impressed many customers with that approach, would we? Instead we offered them more positive assessments. We gave them hope when they needed it most.

"I'm sorry your home was flooded, but we are well trained to handle this sort of thing, and we have specialized equipment to get the job done (confidence). We are certain that we can make things right for you again (optimism) because we've done it for many other homeowners (abundance) over the years."

Now, we only said what we could back up with our best work. Being positive was not a sales pitch, it reflected our capabilities. Our hard work. Our experience. Our specialized tools and talents. Our desire to provide a valuable service to serve a great need.

We prepared and equipped ourselves for success, and that made us all the more optimistic and abundance minded. We believed there were ample opportunities for us to prove our value in the world even with many competitors in our field.

Optimism and abundance drive achievement and create fulfillment. They open your eyes to opportunities and help you not only see the best in others but inspire them to be their best because they want to fulfill the vision you helped them create.

Heroes use their optimistic spirits to inspire and create more heroes. I firmly believe that optimism changes your luck. It changes your perspective from scarcity to abundance. It allows you to rise above the things that hold most people down and provides you the wisdom to respond to situations rather than react to what happens.

I'm sure you've heard references to the pessimistic Murphy's Law, which says that whatever can go wrong will go wrong. I created Brown's addendum to that, which says whatever can go wrong will go wrong—and at the worst possible time.

This phony law is based on pessimism and scarcity. Those who embrace it, often end up experiencing it time and again.

I know this because Lisa and I have sometimes fallen into this chasm of negative thinking. It's easy to do. Like a lot of home-owners, we went through a stretch during which every household appliance broke down just after their warranties expired. You have probably been there. The refrigerator. The washer and dryer. The air-conditioning unit.

We had a fleet of repair trucks in our driveway for weeks. We joked, darkly, that the universe had placed a target on our backs and was out to get us. It seemed like we were fighting a series of uphill battles in every aspect of our lives.

I developed a Murphy's Law mindset, and Lisa's positive spirit was waning. For a bit, we felt the world was piling problem after problem upon us. And then Lisa got us back on track. She realized that other people were dealing with far greater problems than we were.

She replaced thoughts of fear, pessimism, and scarcity with gratitude, optimism, and abundance.

We also learned to adjust our terminology and our attitudes. We turned our attention to solutions instead of problems. We started asking better questions, like how can we create the best outcome with what we have? What can we do right now to move forward? One positive step forward has the capacity to change everything.

This is the secret to both attracting and becoming everyday heroes. Your challenges may seem larger than life, but as someone created to be extraordinary, you have all the superpowers you need.

I'm not talking about walking around proclaiming, "Here I am to save the day!" That's comic-book stuff.

Real-life heroes step up. They don't pose and flex their muscles. They serve by applying their talents and gifts with empathy and kindness to all. They walk into the room and say, "What can I do to help?" "I am here to *serve* today."

True heroes rise above the challenges and adversities of everyday life. They condition themselves to see opportunities in every challenge. You have probably heard the saying "I can't see the forest for the trees."

It's absolutely true. When you're in the thick of a crisis, you can find yourself thinking that bad things only happen to you. The "poor, pitiful me" syndrome seeps into your head.

This self-defeating mentality occurs when you focus on your problems and the negative emotions they stir within you. The hero's secret is to focus on positive actions and solutions, which then opens up opportunities to rise above and beyond.

Let me offer you a true-life example:

As a rugged outdoorsman (wannabe), I drive a big, red, beautiful Chevy Silverado pickup truck. It may be the prettiest truck in the world. I know this because other rugged outdoorsmen (wannabes) tell me that all the time.

Their envy only makes me love my pick-me-up truck even more. And that is why this is such a tragic tale. One day I was sitting in my office having "one of those days."

You know what I mean, right? If I turned right, I should have turned left. If I said yes, I should have said no. If I reached for something on a shelf, I knocked over six other things that fell to the floor and broke.

My karma had crashed and burned. My biorhythms were set on "self-destruction." Murphy's Law was the law of the land.

My team members had disappointed me. Important meetings were cancelled. A big deal did a big belly flop. And a face plant.

By early afternoon, all I could do was sit in my office, stare at the wall, and moan pitifully. Rather than bring down the entire company with my despair, I decided to do a reboot and just go home. Tomorrow will be a new day! I hoped.

I gathered my keys, my day planner, my briefcase, and what remained of my dignity before heading to the parking lot where my big, red, beautiful Chevy Silverado was waiting for me.

Just seeing my pickup perked me up.

I climbed inside the spacious interior, fired up its 6.2-liter engine churning out 420 horses and 460 pounds of torque (whatever that means).

I had a few stops on my way home. Given the disastrous day I'd had so far, I drove with extra caution, as if the pickup bed were loaded with Tiffany crystal vases.

Finally, unscathed, I made it to my last stop. I parked my big, red, beautiful Chevy Silverado. I gave it one last loving look.

Then, as I was walking away from my aforementioned BRBCS, I noticed a woman in her SUV backing out of her parking space. I didn't really think much about it and continued inside.

I hadn't even let go of the door as I heard the horrifying shrieks of metal scraping against metal, followed by the tinkling of shattered glass.

I didn't need to turn around to know what had happened.

I fought the urge to cover my eyes as I walked back outside.

Sure enough, she had backed into my big, red, and formerly beautiful Chevy Silverado.

She had her hands over her eyes, but removed them when she heard me approach. She was whimpering like an abandoned puppy.

Her large and tearful eyes met mine.

She had no idea how bad my day had been up to that point. I wanted to scream, "Where did you learn to drive?"

Also on my scream wish list was, "Did you know there is a mirror in the middle of the windshield that isn't just for applying makeup?"

I did not say any of that, of course.

Here is what I did say: "Hey, it's okay. No one was hurt. That's why we have insurance."

She wept, took a step, and melted into my arms.

She caught me off guard, but it was a good off guard.

Cool! I thought.

I stood there in the driveway, hugging my wife, grateful that I had exhibited a grown-up level of self-control.

Then, because I was a fan of self-help books, I assessed what I could learn from this moment.

Lesson Number One: Never park in such a way that my big, red, beautiful Chevy Silverado pickup is in the path of my wife as she rips out of the garage in her car at a high rate of speed.

Lesson Number Two: Life is not perfect. It is not predictable and bad stuff happens. When it does, we can lose control and make matters worse. Or we can accept it, learn from it, and move on without rancor.

You and I are defined either by what happens to us or by how we respond. When bad stuff happens, as it inevitably does, we can respond with anger and self-pity, or we can respond with acceptance and equanimity (also known as "keeping your cool").

Those who rage and rant and complain when bad stuff happens are self-indulgent and all too eager to put on the V-for-victim hat. You don't want to be around these people, and you certainly don't want to be one of them.

The younger me, the less mature and mad-at-the-world me, would have lost it. I would have made it about me and my truck, instead of focusing on Lisa and her feelings.

You will have a much happier life if you put on the PS-for-problem-solver hat. You know life is pretty darn fair when it comes to dumping bad stuff on every one of us. So you make the choice to look not for pity but for opportunities to make things better.

The choice is always ours to make.

A sense of humor helps too.

Maybe?

A few weeks later, I borrowed several orange caution cones from my neighbor who works for a utility company. Every night, I placed them around my big red beautiful and slightly mangled Chevy Silverado pickup truck.

I thought it was hilarious.

My neighbor thought it was hilarious.

My wife was not amused.

At all.

Optimism Is Like a Muscle

Now, if you don't have access to orange safety cones, you may have difficulty changing your perspective from victim to hero. When bad stuff smacks you upside the head, I suggest you try putting your own challenges aside and try offering to help someone else in need. Stepping up to serve someone else will put you into a more optimistic frame of mind.

The *Good Morning America* anchor Robin Roberts, who has been challenged by breast cancer and a rare blood disorder, once said that optimism is "like a muscle: the more you use it, the stronger it gets."

I believe she is right. Rise up and take control. Optimism and abundance enable you to be the exceptional person you are meant to be. If you are feeling stuck and defeated, here are a few ways you can go from zero to hero:

- Make every person you come into contact feel valued and special.
- Offer to help someone in need by using your unique talents and knowledge.
- Volunteer at a local school, nursing home, church, or community center.
- Join a service organization like the Salvation Army, Red Cross, Rotary Club, Kiwanis, or Best Buddies and participate in their nonprofit programs to serve their communities.
- Take walks in parks and woods, nature preserves, botanical gardens, and other areas where you can experience the healing power of nature.
- Learn meditation and mindfulness methods for clearing your head and adjusting your mood.

Everything Speaks

My friend and branding expert Jeffrey Buntin Jr. helps big business brands tell their stories well. His philosophy and approach to branding is this: "Everything speaks."

When I asked Jeffrey to give me the core of the "everything speaks" philosophy, here is what he said: "'Everything speaks' is about establishing a code with yourself for how you live. It is about synchronizing your values, behaviors, and communication with others. It's about putting the authentic *you* at the center of the life experiences you were meant to have. 'Everything speaks' applies to your personal life, relationships, and to your work."

I agree. Everything and everyone's actions send a message. From the entry-level person at the reception desk to the veteran vice president in her corner office, everyone on your team is a part of your brand's story—good, bad, or otherwise.

Being the brand you represent personally, you need to be aware that your gestures, words, body language, and tone all communicate to the people around you exactly who you are and what you bring to their table.

I believe that "everything speaks" is a vitally important concept. Someone is watching all the time. Not only are they watching, they are locked and loaded, ready to record on a moment's notice and then blitz social media with your magic or misfortune.

I am fascinated when I hear people make excuses for how they act. They will usually recuse themselves from the hot seat by proclaiming something along the lines of "that's just the way I am."

Let me make this crystal clear: the way you are is the way you choose to be. It's absolutely your decision to act the way you do. You may have some genetic predisposition or a life of conditioning that influences your behavior. But make no mistake about it, you are who you are and do what you do because you make the choices that determine your actions.

If you hear friends and family making excuses for you, take the hint. You need to make changes if they have to step in and explain your behavior to others like this:

- She didn't mean to say that.
- He was just venting.
- Her bark is worse than her bite.
- He's been through a lot lately, so cut him some slack.

If people are constantly rising to your defense, you may be offensive. I've known a few folks who say mean and nasty things about others and then claim "I was only being honest."

Yeah, that doesn't cut it either. It's called honesty, not *ho-nasty*. The term comes from the root word "honor," which when used as a verb is a synonym for "respect."

That is a good way to treat people. When you treat others with respect, they respond to you in the same way. And if they don't, so what!?

Be the one who chooses to shine regardless of what someone else does. It's much better for you to rise above. Your example may just plant a seed that begins to grow in someone's life, a seed that gives them hope.

I absolutely believe that we can influence people, yet we may never know the difference we made for them. To treat others honorably and with respect is heroic. It reflects well on them and on you. There's a line from the movie *Batman Begins* that sums it up perfectly: "It's not who you are underneath. It's what you do that defines you." Indeed, everything you do speaks volumes about you.

Don't Suck

A few years ago, I was speaking to a prestigious group of successful entrepreneurs and business owners.

I was nervous, but I've learned to work with it. Being nervous used to slow me down and make me sweat. Now I shift my perspective and use that energy to fire myself up and give a great performance for my audiences.

I was sitting backstage collecting my thoughts and making some last-minute notes. Through the door walked the CEO of the company putting on the event.

He had it going on. Big, tall, and athletic-looking. He was wearing an expensive suit and a nice watch. I don't know what kind of cologne he had on, but it smelled like money.

He walked up to me and introduced himself, extending a hand. (This was back when humans still felt safe shaking hands.) His grip was perfectly firm with just the right amount of knuckle crunch to say, "I'm the boss," without making your knees buckle and your eyes water from the pain.

"I'm really glad you are here, Kevin," he said. "This is a great group of successful people. They need to be inspired to keep doing great things. They also need to be reminded of what got them here and what keeps them here. This is an important message, and I appreciate your being here."

I relaxed a little. I knew he was on my side. He understood what I was about and embraced my story. As he prepared to leave, he put his hand on my shoulder and gave it a little harder squeeze than his handshake.

Only one knee buckled, but he had my full attention.

Then the CEO gave me a look that I'm sure his employees tried to avoid.

Based on that steely look, I braced myself for what was coming.

"Kevin, my man, there is one more thing," the Boss Man said.

"Yes, what is that?"

"Don't suck!"

I like to think he said it with a smile. But I may have made up that part in my mind because I felt myself getting nervous again. Thankfully,

I had learned to transform nervous energy into stage energy, so I went out there and just rocked the gig, as we speaker types say.

The CEO inspired me with his frank and somewhat scary encouragement that day. In fact, whenever I am blessed to take the stage, I hear his gravelly CEO voice and think about those words: *Don't suck.*

People don't care how many times I have been amazing in the past or the number of standing ovations I have received. They don't care what I promise to do in the future. They do expect me to be my very best when I take the stage in front of them. And I owe them that.

I think it's healthy to try to be your best for all the people in your life. Deliver on your promises and raise it a couple of notches. Bring your very best.

Stand and deliver and, most of all, *Don't Suck!*

Heroes own the moments that matter, and they show up every day better than they were yesterday. They bring their best to every endeavor. They never take for granted the blessed opportunity to serve others.

Who can you make feel better today by showing up and giving your best? Whose life can you elevate by taking the time to teach, train, guide, and mentor them? Whose empty bucket can you fill with kindness?

I love that image. I also like to think of everyday heroes as planters, whether in the work place or out in the world. Heroes plant seeds that inspire hope and encouragement. People blossom because of their contributions to their lives.

There's an old saying that if you cut an apple, you can count all of its seeds easily enough. But if you plant those seeds, you can never count all the apples that will grow from them.

So go forth and plant your seeds of hope and encouragement. Be a hero who creates and inspires even more extraordinary people in this world!

12

A HEROIC LEGACY

I HAVE PUT OFF TELLING you this story because it's a sad one in many ways. But it's also inspiring, and I hope that's how you take it. Back in 1996 my then boss, mentor, and hero David called with awful news.

"Kevin, I've got stage IV lung cancer. Doc says I have six months to live."

That may seem blunt, but it was not out of character. David never minced words. He was a straight shooter. He'd tell you exactly how the cow eats the cabbage—the good, the bad, and the ugly.

Still, he sprang that on me so fast, I didn't know what to say at first—a rarity for me. My pause gave David an opportunity to lighten the moment with his wry sense of humor.

"Kevin, the doctor also said I should get a haircut now, because it will be my last one."

All I could get out was: "I am so sorry, buddy."

He wasn't accepting any pity.

"Don't be sorry for me. This just means I need to get to work."

"What are you going to do with six months to live?" I asked, walking into his trap.

"I am going to move in with my mother-in-law. . . . That way I'm assured of the longest six months of my life!"

It's not often a friend calls to tell you he is dying and then he makes you bust out a laugh.

I said, "Quit goofing around, man. What are you going to do?"

"I'm working on myself, Kevin. This didn't just happen. It's the byproduct of poor choices and bad habits. I was arrogant. Thought I was bulletproof. I neglected the fundamentals of good living. This is on me, and now I need to go 'to work.'"

That was the David I knew so well. He always wanted to be better and do better.

"What can I do to help?" I asked.

"Pray."

"Oh, I will, my friend!"

Expect a Miracle

I hung up the phone and melted into a puddle of tears. My mentor and hero was dying. I wanted to help him like he had always helped me, but I had no idea what to do.

My mood was darkening, so I called a mutual friend named Dwight, who was a speaker and mindset coach. I told Dwight about David's cancer diagnosis. His instant response was, "Expect a miracle."

I liked his optimism.

Dwight connected with David and helped our friend prepare his mind and attitude for the battle ahead. The tools he provided included visualization exercises and self-talk strategies.

Dwight had David close his eyes and visualize the cartoon character Yosemite Sam. With guns ablaze, firing blue and green laser beams at every cancer cell in David's body. David was onboard and did everything Dwight asked of him. Unorthodox or not.

David was always a fighter. Now he became a warrior. He walked the talk, displaying all of the tough-mindedness he'd taught me over the years. Standing at death's door, he stood strong. And it seemed to pay off.

It's easy to talk a big game, but David proved he was larger than his challenges. The six months passed. Then a year. Then another.

Over the next ten years, David received four more cancer diagnoses. All of them dire. And none of them stopped him. David and Yosemite Sam were a dynamic duo in their own right. For years David collected figurines and pillows of his friend Sam.

I had to admit that Dwight delivered on the miracle vision when—ten years after David was first told that he had just six months to live—three doctors confirmed that there was no evidence of cancer in his body.

A Final Call

I was so grateful for David's all-clear diagnosis. My friend deserved to enjoy a long life. He'd always been there for me. I might not have stabilized my life, held down a good job, or married a strong woman without his help.

But in 2006, I received another heartbreaking call from my heroic friend.

"Kevin, my cancer is back for a fifth time, and it is back with a vengeance. I am too tired to fight anymore. I'd love to see you before I go."

I packed a suitcase right away and hit the road for the fourteen-hour drive back to Waco. I made it in twelve hours. Don't ask me how. He had sounded exhausted and resigned to dying. I had to get there to say goodbye.

When I walked into David's house, I saw a stranger sitting in his recliner; a dying man, gray of pallor. His voice was just a whisper, but still recognizable. We never forget the voices of influence in our lives.

His was a voice of great influence in my life, after all.

"I'm glad you are home, son," he said.

He reintroduced me to his daughters, who had also rushed to be with him. They helped him out of his chair. He took a couple halting steps to reach me and then hugged me tight. For a dying man, he was still very strong. I felt like he was about to break me in two.

One of the odd things that has stayed with me over the years about that moment: his stubbly beard whiskers, wet with tears, were pressed against my face. He wept as he said, "Now *all* of my kids are here."

David pointed to his back patio.

"Let's go outside and sit for a minute."

We sipped sweet tea and other sipping drinks. We reminisced. We laughed and cried. Two hours of joy and sorrow flew by. And then David went quiet. Sadness overcame his effort to be brave.

He reached over to grab my arm, but missed. I was sitting with my legs crossed and he grabbed my foot instead. He was a proud man and would never want me to know he wasn't actually aiming for my foot. So he just held my foot.

David struggled to say something. Choking on his emotions. Tearing up again. His whole body was shaking. Then, in a quivering voice, he willed the words out of his mouth: "I am proud of you, Kevin."

We never outgrow the need to hear those powerful words. I most certainly had not.

"I love you, and I am going to miss you."

David then sat back and said, "I just want to know that it mattered, Kevin."

"That what mattered?"

"I just want to know that my time on earth mattered—that it counted for something. Will anyone even know I was here? Did I work hard enough? Did I serve enough? Did I give enough? Did I love enough? Because right now, I'm not so sure. I am about to meet my maker, and I can't get one minute back. I can't change one thing that I did or didn't do."

He took a deep breath, and after a long exhale, he said, "I don't know. I guess it doesn't really matter now."

I put my hand on his shoulder.

"Listen to me," I said softly. "I wouldn't even be here today without you. I owe you everything. You mattered."

I squeezed his shoulder and leaned toward him.

"I love you, David. I am going to miss you for sure. But it's time for you to rest. You did enough. You left a mark that cannot be erased. You are my best friend. My mentor. My coach. Thank you for being my other dad."

In our day-to-day scrambles, we often neglect to ask those same questions about our own lives. "Did I do enough? Did I show up better today than I did yesterday? Did I make life better for those around me?"

But in the end, don't we all want to make a difference in this world? To leave the people in our life better than we found them? Most of us don't think about making a lasting mark as we move through the fleeting moments of our lives, but I encourage you to keep the end in mind. What will linger when you leave?

You can leave a legacy through kindness, encouragement, sharing knowledge, and listening to understand the needs and desires of others. After you take your last breath, someone will probably summarize your entire life in a few words at a memorial service. What will they say about you? How will you be remembered?

That is up to you, in every minute of every day that you have left on this earth. Heroes and mentors live their legacies every day as they pour a little bit of themselves into those around them. That is why heroes never really die. They live on in the hearts and minds and actions of those they have influenced.

Healing Relationships

Around the time that I lost David, another person came into my life as a force for healing. I should say, "She came back into my life." She is a major part of my legacy, and I hope to be a major part of hers as well.

No one should ever leave this earth without healing important relationships that, for whatever reason, were damaged or lost. That thought led me to seek forgiveness and healing with my daughter, the child I'd lost at an early age because of my divorce and a lack of resources.

I was nineteen when she was born. A few years later, I kissed her tiny forehead and said goodbye. As I walked away, my prayers for forgiveness began and continued over all the years. I hoped for redemption one day.

Thankfully, she grew into a woman who believes in second chances and new beginnings. She is a remarkable young woman blessed with heroic kindness.

We reconnected online just after her eighteenth birthday in 2006. Nervous and hopeful, I had registered with an online service for birthparents in search of their children. An "angel" from Texas saw my information and made the connection to help us find each other.

Three years later, we met in person. This marked the first time I'd seen her since I kissed her forehead and said goodbye. I had missed her so much. But I had made a promise that I would stay away.

"Beautifully awkward" would describe our first get together. I was a bundle of nerves wrapped around a nest of butterflies. She was likely feeling the same way.

We've taken many steps together since that first meeting. Some sideways. Some of them backwards. But mostly straight ahead.

I invited her to come to a speaking engagement in Michigan a few years ago. As I took the stage I saw her in the back of the room. She gave me a quiet wave and a smile. I'm pretty sure my heart stopped for a second.

I have no idea what I said in that speech, or if the audience enjoyed it. I do know it was the greatest moment on stage for me. Just having her there.

I am so proud of her and the strong person she has become. Our relationship continues to grow. I am grateful for her willingness to write this chapter of our story together.

She is a gift in my life, one I don't deserve. She also is a tribute to her mother and the adoptive father who raised her. I am grateful to them for giving her the life I could not provide when she first entered the world. I owe them a debt I could never repay.

My daughter has given me the gift of her forgiveness and the even greater gift of a grandchild. Yes, I am papa to a sweet little girl. My granddaughter is pure sunshine and joy. She owns a large chunk of my heart, and I know one day she will brighten the world, just as she has brought her light to my life.

I am so thankful to have found healing with her. My hope is that you will have the opportunity to mend any lost relationships as well. It may take exceptional strength and maybe even professional help, but you will be a better person for it.

Give Yourself a Shot at an Extraordinary Life

Time moves so swiftly, so don't wait until tomorrow to be your best and do your best. Now is the time to discover your best possible self, show up every day, and choose *not* to be ordinary. Now is the time to help people—with no strings attached. Don't wait to create an exceptional experience for the people you serve.

Take responsibility for your attitude, actions, and results right now. View the world through the lens of optimism. If you do these things, I am absolutely convinced it will change your life. And maybe even change the world around you.

Our world needs your unique abilities, your superpowers, and the best that is within you—the talents, gifts, and abilities that are uniquely yours. I certainly want to make a positive impact on your life.

With this book, I hope I've done a little for you of what David did for me.

David couldn't force me to change my perspective, but he always reminded me that it was far better to look forward than to look back. He kept me on track and helped me correct my course along the way.

"You have to decide to put in the work if you want to do better and be better," he would tell me. "I can't do that for you."

He made me take responsibility for those things I could control and let go of those I could not control. Many times, I've watched people who are unwilling to do the work. They just want the result.

As David used to say: "Before you can be the noun you have to be the verb."

They want better lives with greater rewards but without any more effort. They aren't willing to work on their characters, their relationships, and their attitudes. And as a result, they leave nothing behind but unfulfilled potential. They were born to be extraordinary but settled for much less.

Through the kindness of David and others, I came to understand that I would keep getting the same results unless I changed my ways. Now is a good time to go to work on yourself to become the best possible version of yourself: a hero in your own life story and a hero to those within your reach.

Back to the Mirror

"The beginning is the end and the end is the beginning," David often told me.

He meant that whenever you set out to achieve a goal, you should have a vision of where you want to end up. I found this very helpful in keeping me focused on what I wanted to achieve, even when challenges arose.

David also said that when you achieve any goal, your question always should be, "What's next?"

The answer of course is "another beginning."

So let's end where we began.

My hero's journey began with a look in the mirror. Lisa encouraged me to look there for all of those people who have made my life better. These gracious and patient men and women helped to make me better than I could have been without their guidance.

When I was saying goodbye to David, we sat and reflected upon life. At one point, when his emotions overcame him and he sat with his head in his hands, I leaned in and whispered, "What is it friend?"

"I'm scared, KB," he said. "Really scared."

"David, you don't have to be scared to let go. You know this ends with a new beginning. Don't be afraid to die."

He turned to me, tilted his head slightly and said, "I'm not afraid to die, son. Not for one minute am I afraid to die. But after sixty-four years on this planet I am scared to death that I never lived."

"I'm scared that I didn't show up for the people and moments when I could have made a difference," he added. "I'm scared that I was racing through life on autopilot half the time and the other half chasing something that turns out was right in front of me the whole time. I'm scared, son, that after all those years, no one will even know I was here."

His words broke my heart. This guy not only changed my life but also saved it. Then on death's door he wondered if anyone would remember him.

I remember him. And now, you will, too.

David taught me a final life lesson before he died.

He looked at me and said, "Son, don't make the same mistakes that I did. I'm not going to be here to remind you of what we learned together."

My friend cleared his throat, squared his shoulders, and summoned his best deep baritone. "As long as there's a breath in your body, son, you have work to do. As long as there's a breath in your body there is a version of you that you haven't even met yet. A version the rest of the world desperately needs. Don't you dare be so selfish that you take the best of you to the grave."

His words left me speechless. The weight of words can pierce the heart in good ways and bad. David had given me so much.

I reminded him of something he taught me many years before. He always told me that the people who cross our paths in life come to us for a purpose. Not by accident or coincidence, but by assignment.

They are sent to you because of who you are, not what you do or what you own. And the only way you can truly honor and serve them is to give them the gift of your full attention. Give them your best and help them be their best.

I really wrote this book to ask you the two questions David always asked me.

1. Can you look in the mirror and see the faces of those who helped you become who you are today? Those who poured their best into you and left you better than they found you? If so, do me a favor and remember them. Honor them in all that you do. In fact, when you're done reading this, call one of them and thank them, before you can't.

2. But here's the big one: Who looks in the mirror and sees *your* face? Who is better because you showed up for them? Because you gave them a smile. Because you listened to their stories. Because you encouraged them when life was beating down on them. Who is better because you were there for them?

You never know when or why someone will look to you as a friend, a mentor, or a hero. The next person may have just left the doctor with a diagnosis they didn't see coming. Perhaps their marriage just blew up and now they're alone. Maybe, they just put a child in rehab and they are at the end of their rope.

The truth is, you don't know what you don't know, so give everyone you meet the best you have to offer. Your willingness to listen to them, grieve with them, guide them, and encourage them will determine your own legacy.

This world needs heroes willing to unleash their best in each moment and pour their gifts into the lives of others.

This is your time to make a contribution and leave a mark that cannot be erased. The world needs you to be a hero, now more than ever.

Like the sign in my office says, "Always be yourself . . . unless you can be Batman. Then you should always be Batman."

• ACKNOWLEDGMENTS •

Nothing significant can be accomplished alone. A lot of people helped make this book possible.

To all of my friends and family, thank you for being in my corner. For loving me when I was unlovable. Helping me when I couldn't help myself. And for giving me grace when I didn't deserve it.

This book would not have become a reality without my friend and business manager, Michele Lucia, and the ADL Speaker Management team; my literary agent, Shannon Marven, and her staff at Dupree-Miller; Tim Burgard and the HarperCollins Leadership family; and finally, my alter ego and writing partner, Wes Smith, who helped bring this book to life in ways I never imagined.

You are all heroes in my book.

· ABOUT THE AUTHOR ·

Kevin Brown understands what drives organizational excellence and customer loyalty. He knows firsthand how great brands think, feel, and act. He is a branding and culture expert with a career in franchise development that spans thirty years.

Kevin helped build a little-known family business into the No. 1 brand in their industry with revenues reaching $2 billion. Along the way, he learned how to overcome adversity, deal with change, and create a culture that drives extraordinary results in business and in life.

In 2017, Kevin retired from corporate America to take his message around the world. Today, he is recognized as one of the best inspirational speakers in the world. His keynote messages have been delivered to hundreds of thousands of people worldwide. You can learn more at KevinBrownSpeaks.com.